THE

ROCK-TEMPLES

OF

ELEPHANTA OR GHÂRÂPURÎ,

DESCRIBED AND ILLUSTRATED

BY

J. BURGESS, M. R. A. S., F. R. G. S.

GYAN

Published by

GYAN

Gyan Publishing House
5, Ansari Road
Daryaganj, New Delhi-110002
Phone: 011-47034999, 9811692060
E-mail: books@gyanbooks.com

Distribution Network
gyanbooks.com
India, USA, Canada, UK, Australia, France

ISBN: 978-81-212-7939-0 (PB)
First Published, 1871

2nd Impression 2023

Printed at: Gyan Press, Delhi.

THE ROCK-TEMPLES OF ELEPHANTA OR GHÂRÂPURÎ
Author: J. BURGESS

THE ROCK-TEMPLES OF ELEPHANTA OR GHÂRÂPURÎ

I. ENTRANCE TO THE GREAT TEMPLE.

P. I.

THE

ROCK-TEMPLES

OF

ELEPHANTA OR GHÂRÂPURÎ,

BY

J. BURGESS, M.R.A.S., F.R.G.S.,

WITH

PHOTOGRAPHIC ILLUSTRATIONS BY D. H. SYKES.

BOMBAY:

D. H. SYKES & Co.—THACKER, VINING & Co.

1871.

CONTENTS.

PLANS, &c.

PHOTOGRAPHS.

ELEPHANTA IN 1579.

"The Pagodes and Images are many and innumerable throughout the Orientall countries.............There is yet another Pagode which they hold and esteem for the highest and chiefest Pagode of all the rest, which standeth in a little Iland called Pory: this Pagode by the Portingals is called the Pagode of the Elephant. In that Iland standeth an high hill, and on the top thereof there is a hole, that goeth down into the hill, digged & carved out of the hard rock or stones as big as a great cloyster: within it hath both places and cesternes for water, very curiously made, and round about the wals are cut out & formed, the shapes of Elephâts, Lions, Tigers, and a thousand other such like wilde and cruel beasts: also some Amazones and many other deformed thinges of divers sorts, which are so well and workmanlike cut, that it is strange to behold. It is thought that the Chinos (which are verie ingenious workmen) did make it, when they used to traffique in the Countrie of India. These Pagodes and buildings are now whollie left overgrowne, and spoyled since the Portingales had it under their subjections. By these places may it bee coniectured that their Pagodes are still within the land, even till this day, speciallie where the kings and governours are all of that religion, and keepe their Courtes and Palaces."

JOHN HUIGHEN VAN LINSCHOTEN,

Discours of Voyages into ye Easte and West Indies, Boke, I. ch. 44.

ELEPHANTA ROCK TEMPLE.

PLAN.

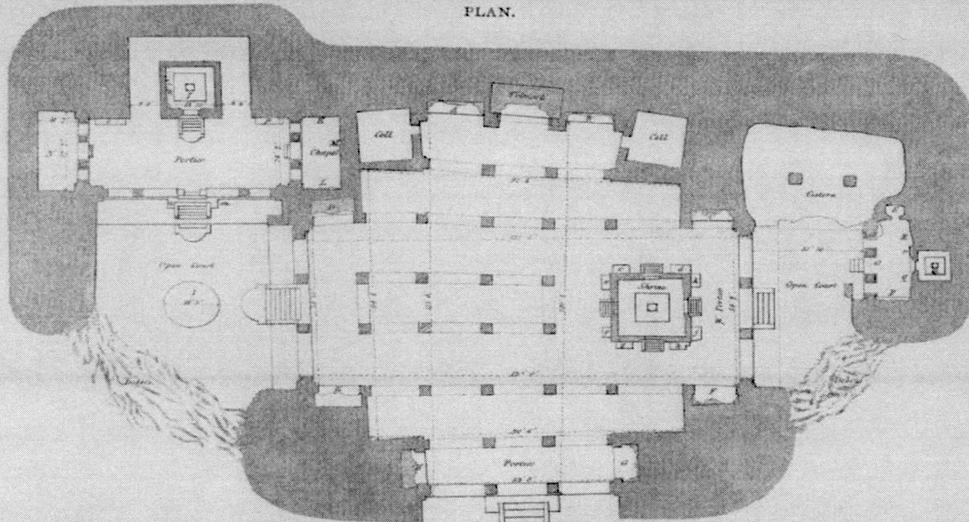

J. Burgess delt.

Scale of feet.

W. GRIGGS, PHOTO LITH. LONDON. S. E.

THE ROCK TEMPLES

OF

ELEPHANTA OR GHÂRÂPURÎ.

INTRODUCTION.

FEW visitors to Bombay, possessed of any curiosity or liking for antiquities, neglect the opportunity of seeing the famous Hindu rock-cut temple of Elephanta. But on entering it, the stranger, not conversant with Hindu mythology, feels the want of some guide to explain the meaning of those gigantic and monstrous mutilated statues with their surrounding sculptures that fill the various compartments of the walls. They have been several times described,[1]* but these accounts are not generally known or accessible, and the want of a separate description is much felt.

2. The island of Elephanta, or Ghárápurí[2] as it is called by the Hindus, is about six miles from Bombay, and four from the shore of the mainland. Having a circumference of about four or four and a half miles, it consists of two long hills with a narrow valley between them that opens out somewhat to the south-east. It is covered chiefly with low *Karandá*† bushes, interspersed with *Táḍ*‡ or Palmyra palm and other trees, and at certain seasons is very unhealthy. It was named *Elephanta* by the Portuguese, from a large stone elephant that stood near the old landing place on the south side of the island.[3] This elephant was 13 feet 2 inches in length and about 7 feet 4 inches high, but its head and neck dropped off in September 1814, and subsequently the body sunk down into a shapeless mass of stones, which in 1864 were removed to the Victoria Gardens in Bombay.

3. To the north of a ruined Portuguese building and about where the two

---

* The notes have been mostly numbered, and will be found appended at the end of the description.

† Carissa Caranda. ‡ Borassus flabelliformis.

hills approach each other, not far to the south-east of the great cave, there was also formerly the statue of a horse carved in stone, "so lively," says Ovington writing in 1689, "with such a colour and carriage, and the shape finisht with that "Exactness, that many have rather fancyed it, at a distance, a living Animal, "than only a bare Representation."[4] Captain Hamilton, however, thought it "not so proportionable and well shaped as the Elephant."[5] It seems to have disappeared between 1712, when Captain Pyke saw it, and 1764 when Niebuhr visited the island.

4. The landing place is now on the north-west of the island, where a paved ascent constructed in 1853-54[6] leads up from the shore to the front of the great cave, but at low water boats have to lie out at a considerable distance from the shore.

THE GREAT ROCK-TEMPLE.

5. The excavations that have been finished, or nearly so, are four,—a fifth is a large cave now much filled up, with only rough masses of stone left to support the roof; and a sixth is merely the beginning of the front of what seems to have been intended for a very small excavation—possibly two or three cells for recluses. But none of them are much visited except the Great Cave. It is in the western hill of the island and at an elevation of about 250 feet above high-water level. It faces the north, and is entirely hewn out of a hard compact species of trap rock. The rock has also been cut away on either side, leaving open areas affording entrances from its east and west sides. Mr. Fergusson describes it as of the general form now known as a *chaori*, or nuptial hall, and bearing a singular resemblance in size, plan and detail to the Dumar Lena, one of the finest of the Elura caves.[7]

6. The principal entrance—indeed the only one that can now be said to be quite open—faces the north; and were the earth removed, which in the course of ages has accumulated up to the level of the floor, it would add to the effect of the first view of this stupendous cave by revealing the basement on which the temple stands, with an ascent by steps each two and a half feet broad, leading up to the central opening of the three in the façade. Over this entrance is a thick mass of nearly perpendicular rock overhung by small trees and shrubs. The impression on the mind may be imagined rather than described when one enters the portico, passing from the glare and heat of tropical sunshine to the dim light and cooler air of the temple, and realizes that he is under a vast roof of solid rock that seems to be supported only by the ranges of massive columns that recede in the vistas on every side, and some of which appear to have split or fallen under the tremendous superincumbent weight; and the feeling of strange uncertain awe that creeps over the mind is only prolonged when in the obscure

light we begin to contemplate the gigantic stony figures ranged along the walls from which they seem to start and from the living rock of which they are hewn.

7. The view from the front of the cave is one of exceeding beauty, commanding the fine bay between Elephanta, Trombay, and the mainland. From the grey dawn of morning till the shades of night close down upon it, whether crowded with the white sails of hundreds of fishing craft, or only marked here and there by one or two passenger boats, and perhaps a small steamer, it is an ever fresh and varying scene of beauty. And a few steps from the porch will lead the visitor to the site of an old bangala, which commands the prospect, to the south-west, of Bombay and its splendid harbour, with Butcher Island in the foreground. Any true lover of Nature will feel himself amply rewarded for his trouble by the magnificent views to be here enjoyed.

8. The accompanying ground plan will convey the best general idea of the form and arrangement of the parts of the cave. From the front entrance to the back it measures about 130 feet, and its length from the east to the west entrance is the same. It does not, however, occupy the entire square of this area. What may be called the porticos on the three open sides are only about 54 feet long and 16½ feet deep. Omitting these and the back aisle, immediately in front of three of the principal sculptured compartments, which is of about the same dimensions as each portico, we may consider the body of the cave as a square of about 91 feet each way, supported by six rows of columns with six columns in each row,—except at the corners, and where the uniformity is broken on the west side to make room for the shrine or *Sacellum*, which occupies a space equal to that enclosed by four of the columns. The plan shows very distinctly too the irregularities of the dimensions—irregularities that do not at first sight strike the eye, but which prevail in most cave-temples. By actual measurement it is found that scarcely two columns are exactly alike in the sizes of even their principal details, and often are not even square, nor three of them in a line. The angles at the corners differ considerably from right angles, and the depth of the cave as well as its height varies very considerably in the east and west sides.

9. The porticos have each two pillars and two pilasters or demi-columns in front. The columns are very massy, and were originally twenty-six in number with sixteen half columns. But eight of the separate pillars have been destroyed and others are much injured. As neither the floor nor the roof are perfectly horizontal, they vary in height from 15 to 17 feet. The aisle at the back has a chamber at each end of it 16 feet by 17½ or 18 feet. The portico on the east side opens into a court, from which an ascent of a few steps on the south leads into a smaller cave, whose extreme dimensions, however, are 89 feet in length by 56 in depth. It consists of an open veranda with open chapels at each end, and a shrine or *adytum* at the back, with a *pradakshina* or passage for circumambulation, about eight and a half feet wide, quite round it. At the other end of the

great hall is also an open court with a large water-cistern on the south side, of which a large portion of the roof has fallen in, and with other debris now almost quite fills it up; and at the west side of this court is a small open chapel with a *linga* shrine at the back.

10. The principal architectural feature of this and of nearly all other cave temples is the pillars. Mr. Fergusson, the greatest authority on Indian architecture, thinks that while most of the details in the rock excavations of this country are mere repetitions in stone of the wooden forms prevalent in the civil architecture of the age when they were first cut, the pillars are an exception to this rule, and "seem never to have been of wood," yet he admits that in one of the oldest examples he can adduce "the capital is merely a wooden ornament repeated in stone."[8] Now in very many of the earlier caves the pillars are plain octagons without base or capital,—one of the most natural forms into which to fashion wooden pillars; and even where they become more elaborately carved there is no difficulty in matching them with the wooden columns in many of the Jaina temples of Gujarat and even in modern Hindu houses. It was to be expected, however, that immediately that pillars came to be carved in the more brittle material of stone they would be considerably increased in diameter, which again would admit of new forms of mouldings, so that the original wooden prototypes would be early lost sight of. And after the cutting of Rock Temples had been practised for eight, or ten, or more centuries it could scarcely be expected that in those of Elephanta we should find the traces of such originals very distinctly marked: still it would not be very difficult, were this the place, to show by existing examples the gradual transformation of wooden forms into the Elephanta type of column. These pillars have not all exactly the same dimensions and proportions,—but as in the example represented in the figure,—we have in all—first a square shaft about 3 feet 4 inches each way rising to nearly half the total height or 8 feet, the upper 16 inches of which is bound about as it were by a band of very slight projection; the next 2 inches is octagonal, and on the shoulders thus formed, on all the columns within the *square* of the temple and on those of the west porch, sit small figures of *Ganesha* or some other *deva*. Above this 7 inches has shallow flutes—thirty-two in the circumference, and the next 6 inches in height is octagonal. From this springs the fluted neck of the column 3 feet in length, and diminishing from 3 feet 1 inch to 2 feet 9 inches, the flutes ending in projecting cusps under a thin beaded torus, and over this a second line of cusps project and curve outwards under a thin fillet. On this again rests the compressed-cushion shaped capital 1 foot 9½ in. thick, and projecting about 16 inches beyond the face of the pillar; the middle of this capital is bound by a narrow flat band breaking its sixty-four flutes. Above is a circular neck 3 inches deep and then a square plinth of the same width as the base, and about 8 inches deep. This last and the abacus or bracket it supports are plainly enough imitations of wooden details. The bracket slopes away upwards on each side to the architrave

ELEPHANTA.

II. Column in the Great Cave.

See § 10.

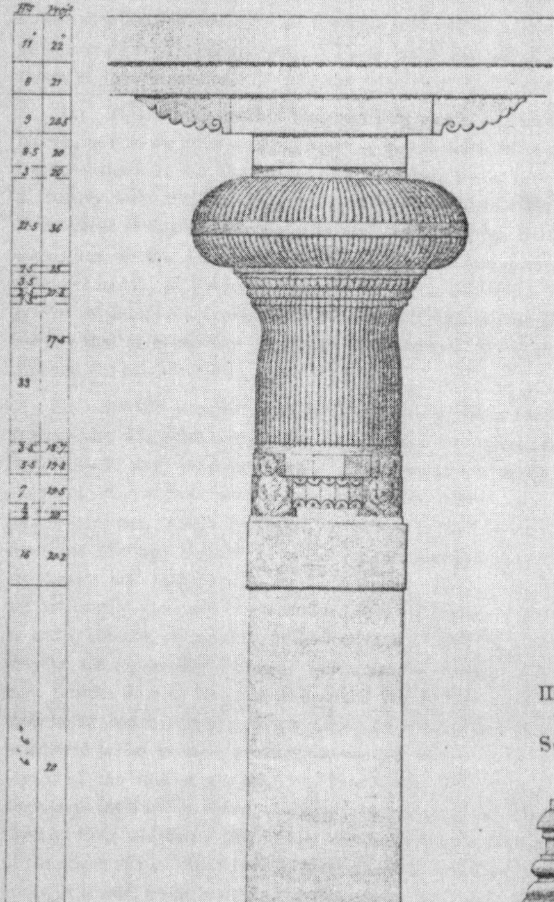

III. Base under the Sculptures.

§ 11

Scale of 12 6 0 1 2 3 4 5 6 7 feet.

J. Burgess, delt.

Government Litho. Press, Bombay 1871.

in a series of fanciful scrolls divided, or connected, by a band over their middle. The architraves—also imitations of wooden beams—run generally from east to west across the cave—the exceptions being the lintels over the east and west entrances, and those connecting the two inner pillars of the east portico, and the two pillars in front of the east face of the shrine. In the latter case the architraves are returned so as not to run in above the shrine.

11. Almost the only other architectural features are the door jambs and the bases under the front and sides of the main cave and its adjuncts and under some of the sculptured compartments. These latter are all of one pattern,—that shown in the illustration.

12. This temple has not been regularly used as a place of worship for generations, nor do we know certainly when or why it ceased to be so used, but it is at least probable that the Portuguese, in their fanatical zeal against the Hindu form of idolatry, desecrated the temple in the early part of the sixteenth century ?[9] Still on occasions of Shaiva festivals it is used, especially by Hindus of the Banian caste; and at the *Shivarátri* festival—just before the first new moon* falling after the middle of February—a religious fair is held here. Now as this is the greatest of the *Shaiva* festivals, the occurrence of this fair at Elephanta seems to indicate that it must once have been the principal, if not the oldest, temple of *Shiva* in the neighbourhood.

13. But the stranger must not forget that a Hindu temple has very little analogy to a Christian church: it is not a place for public prayer, or religious instruction in any recognised form. Except perhaps on a few special occasions, there are not even fixed hours for the ceremonials. Every one goes as it suits his own convenience, repeats his prayer, prostrates himself before the idol, and lays down his offering: if there is a fair he goes out into the crowd and purchases sweetmeats and perhaps toys for his children. His ideas in coming to worship are not usually—scarcely ever connected with his neglect of duty, his deficiencies in truth, honesty, or morality, or the expiation of the guilt of such offences. His prayers are regarded as charms or spells, and his offerings as bribes that his god may prosper him in his undertakings and satisfy his wishes—without regard to these being honourable or selfish, virtuous or criminal and vicious. The worship is believed to be in itself meritorious—an *opus operatum* in fact—and therefore worthy of the utmost attention on the part of the worshipper; hence those devoted to his worship spare no pains in performing the ceremonies required of them by their *shástras*. The nature of this worship is illustrated by the legend of the origin of the *Shivarátri*[10] festival given in the Bhavishya Purána. A forester, it is said, being benighted in the woods the night before the new moon of Phálguna, took refuge in a *Bilva* tree, and kept awake by the fear of wild beasts,

* The day before the commencement of Phalguna Shuddha.

he involuntarily observed the *jágarana* or vigil of the season. Having nothing to eat he was obliged to keep the fast; and throwing down twigs of the tree, some of them fell on a deserted *linga* near its foot, and thus he unwittingly performed the prescribed offering. Being destroyed next day by a tiger, the messengers of *Yama* came to carry off his spirit to the infernal regions, but were opposed by the servants of *Shiva*, who—merely because of his involuntary observance of the *Shivarátri* rites—claimed him as theirs, and carried him off in triumph. Hence the observance of this ritual is considered as an expiation of all sins, a means of attaining all desires in this life and final liberation in the next.

14. Nor do the Hindus all worship the same gods. Their Aryan ancestors worshipped the powers of nature personified,—such as *Indra*, the god of thunder and rain; *Varuna*, the god of the sky; *Agni*, the god of fire; *Mitra*, the sun; *Ushas*, the dawn; the *Maruts* or winds; *Rudra*, the god of storms; &c. But perhaps as far back as the Christian era those who were not Buddhists began to introduce new gods, and to connect the names and appellations of the old gods with new and greatly degraded characters. And by the eighth century, these had attained the supremacy; their followers persecuted the Buddhists, and somewhat later seem to have exterminated them. The Brahmans—the creators and self-constituted priests of these new gods—of course acquired unlimited influence over the minds of the people. But even Brahmans differed about the god entitled to highest worship and his character; and so there are at least six distinct sects,—1. The *Shaivas* who worship Shiva; 2. The *Vaiṣhnavas* who regard Viṣhnu as supreme; 3. The *Sauryas* or worshippers of Súrya—the sun; 4. The *Gánapatyas* devoted to Ganpati or Ganesha—the elephant-headed god of wisdom; 5. The *Sháktas* who adore Bhaváni or Párváti—the *Shakti* of Shiva—the goddess of nature, in her various forms; and 6. The *Bhágavatas* who recognise all the five divinities equally. But the great mass of the people belong to the *Shaiva*, *Vaiṣhnava*, or *Shákta* sects. Each sect again is divided into different schools: thus, the exclusive *Shaivas* allow no worship to be paid to Viṣhnu,[11] but the *Smárttas* though they maintain the supremacy of Shiva above all the other gods, yet direct them also to be worshipped in subordination to him.

15. Now as all the sculptures relate to this *Shiva*, in order to understand them we must attend to his history. Etymologically his name implies 'he of whom growth, increase, or prosperity is,' and he is the personification of the productive power of nature,—hence, in some respects, not unlike *Savitṛí* (the progenitor) of the Vedas. He is called the 'Wearer of the Eight Forms,' as being identified with Earth, Water, Air, Fire, Ether, the Sun, the Moon, and the Sacrificer;* he rides on the bull called *Nandí* as his *váhána* or vehicle, just as *Indra* is borne by

* Colebrooke, *Essays* vol. II. p. 248. Sometimes the last three are identified as Mind, Individuality, and Crude Matter.

the elephant *Airavati*, and *Bhaváni* on her tiger: he has many names as *Ísha* or *Ishwara*, *Maheshwara*, *Rudra*, *Hara*, *Shankara*, *Shambhu*,[12] *Mahádeva* or *Mahesha*, *Mahábaleshwara*,* *Trilochan*[13], *Shriranga*,† *Bhútanátha* or *Bhútesha*,—the lord of demons, &c.—a thousand in all.[14] His crest is the new moon—sometimes described as a third eye, though this eye is distinct from the crescent and is placed vertically in the brow. His usual symbol is a *trishula* or trident; and he is abundantly decked with serpents, wearing them as a necklace, as ear-rings,‡ about his wrists, arms, waist, &c.; and he is often represented with a pendent collar of human sculls.‖ Sometimes he is represented with two hands, at others with four, eight, or ten, and with five faces; besides the *trishula* he often holds in one of his hands the *pasha*—a rope or noose for binding and strangling those with whom he is offended, in another the *gadha* or *parasha*—a battle club, and in a third an antelope or hare *(Mrigu)*, whilst *Ganga* or the Ganges is represented as a female head among his hair. His loins are wrapped in a tiger skin. His appropriate seat is *Mount Kailasa*,—every splinter of whose rocks is an inestimable gem; and his terrestrial haunts are among the lofty *Himálaya*, whence flow the great rivers that fertilize Hindustan, and from this he takes the title of *Girisha*—'Lord of the Mountains,' and thus probably he absorbed the Vedic name of Rudra§ 'god of storms,' whilst his wife is *Párvati*—'the mountain-born,' and *Durgá*—'daughter of mountains.' Associated with the eternal snows of these mountains, he was viewed as a penitent or ascetic, and the chief of ascetics, with a great many corresponding names.[15] This penance he is fabled to have begun on the death of his consort *Sati*, the daughter of *Daksha*, who put an end to herself from grief because she and her husband were not invited to a great sacrifice her father made, and to which he invited all the other gods.

16. Originally Shiva was most probably a popular god of the aboriginal tribes of the Dekhan, but adopted by the Brahmans under the designation of *Mahádeva* or the great god,[16] the Sun-god, the source of nourishment, fertility, and increase, and by those of the south especially he was invested with the triple functions of creation, preservation, and destruction or change. To him are sacred the *Ashoka*¶ shrub—remarkable for its exquisite beauty when in full bloom; the *Nirgundi***; and the *Bilva*,†† also known by the names of *Malura* and *Shriphul*—of the flowers of which Shiva alone wears a chaplet, and which are offered to him only and to no other god. And lastly, his symbol and most frequent form of image is the *Linga*, identical with the ithyphallic emblem of ancient Egypt

---

* That is "Lord of Great Power"; the hill sanatarium in the south of the Bombay Presidency derives its name from this title of Shiva.

† From this is derived *Shrirangapattam*—the name of the capital of Maisur, corrupted by the English into Seringapatam.

‡ Hence called *Nágkundala*.

‖ Called *Rundmálá*.

§ From *Párvata* a mountain.

¶ The *Jonesia Asoca*; conf. Asiat. Jour. 1816, Vol. II. pp. 545-46.

** *Vitex Negundo* or *trifolia*.

†† *Ægle marmelos* or *cratæva religiosa*.

and Greece.[17] From this symbol the Shaiva worshippers of southern India take the name of *Lingáits*.[18] When it was first adopted, however, it is very difficult to say; it is not mentioned in any of the Vedic hymns or Brahmanas—the most ancient religious books of the Hindus; and it is only when we come to the great epics—the *Mahábhárata* and *Rámáyana*,[19] that we find it alluded to. It seems very probable, however, that it was received with the worship from the aboriginal tribes. In favour of the non-Aryan origin of *Shiva* and his worship, we have the entire difference of character and position in the Pantheon between the *Rudra* of the Vedic writings and the *Shiva* of the Purános; then in the legend of *Daksha*, the ancient sages are represented as considering *Shiva* without any claim to a portion in the sacrifice and unwilling to allow him any share, whilst *Shiva*, desirous to have a portion, speaks of it as 'the former practice' and 'contrivance 'of all the gods that in all sacrifices no portion should be divided to him,' and he tells *Devi* that, 'in his sacrifice, his worshippers adore him in the sacrifice of 'devotion, *without a Brahman*, and in this they offer him his portion;' and in the violent destruction of the sacrifice by *Shiva* and the subsequent submission of *Daksha* to him together with the promise of *Brahmá* that *Shiva* shall henceforth have a share in the sacrifice,[20]—we have probably more than a hint at the supersession of the older Vedic worship by the rites of *Shiva*. Again in the *Linga*[21] and other *Puránas* a dispute arises between *Brahmá* and *Vishnu* as to which of them is supreme, when *Shiva* appears as a flaming *linga* and claims and asserts his superiority to them both, and, according to some accounts, even cuts off one of *Brahmá's* heads to punish his falsehood:[22]—this also is perhaps a mythical version of a contest for superiority between the old and new forms of worship. And further, as remarked by Stevenson,—in the Dekhan, "no Brahman officiates in a *Linga* temple. The Brahmans alone officiate as image dressers in the temples of *Vishnu*, and of all the gods connected with the ancient Brahmanical worship; but for the temples of the *Linga*, a distinct order of men, originally of Shudra origin, have been set apart and form now a separate caste under the name *Guravá*. The *Guravá* dresses the image and takes care of the temple; and all that the Brahman or any other worshipper does, is to present before the image his offering of dry rice, plantains, flowers, turmeric, &c., not interfering with the *Guravá's* dispositions or touching the image. It is quite contrary, however, when a Brahman worshipper comes to *Vishnu*; he displaces the drooping flowers if he pleases, and places on the image fresh ones with sandal-wood paste, —a liberty he may not take with *Mahádeva*." In Gujarat also *Báwás* or *Yogis* are frequently the ministrant priests of the Shaiva temples. Lastly, the worship of *bhúts* or demons is still practised by aboriginal tribes and low castes, and *Shiva* is called *Bhútanátha* and *Bhútesha*,—another indication of his aboriginal origin.

17. In the *Kumára Sambhava*, a Sanskrit poem, written probably in an age when the worship of *Shiva* had first risen to eminence, and before it had been developed and debased in the form we now find it, the poet thus describes him:—

> "Refuge of worlds, O how should *Shiva* deign
> To look on men enslaved to paltry gain?
> The spring of wealth himself, he careth nought
> For the vile treasures that mankind have sought;
> His dwelling place amid the tombs may be,
> Yet Monarch of three great worlds is he;
> What though no love his outward form may claim
> The stout heart trembles at his awful name;
> Who can declare the wonders of his might,
> The trident-wielding god, who knows aright?
> Whether around him deadly serpents twine;
> Or if his jewelled wreaths more brightly shine;
> Whether in rough and wrinkled hide arrayed,
> Or silken robe in glittering folds displayed,—
> If on his brow the crescent moon he bear,
> Or if a shrunken skull be withering there!
> The funeral ashes touched by him acquire
> The glowing lustre of eternal fire;
> Falling in golden showers, the Heavenly Maids
> Delight to pour them on their shining braids.
> What though no treasures fill his storehouse full,
> What though he ride upon his horned bull;
> Not e'en may *Indra* in his pride withhold
> The lowly homage that is his of old,—
> But turns his raging elephant to meet
> His mighty lord, and bows before his feet,
> Right proud to colour them rich rosy red
> With the bright flowers that deck his prostrate head."[23]

Such were the elevated expressions of the ideas of the cultivated poet, but, as in all analogous cases, the unhappiness was that he who gave utterance to sayings so beautiful as those we find scattered up and down in this fine poem, and they who admired them, did no more than admire,—while the common herd of men never even heard of them, and their ideas were doubtless, as they have ever been elsewhere, vastly lower—the outgrowth of man's sin-darkened and foolish heart.

18. This temple then, like all the other Brahmanical Rock Temples in Western India, is a *Shaiva* one, and, according to Dr. Stevenson, it belongs to the *Smártta* school of that sect.[24] It is possible, however, that it may be older than the present divisions of the sect, and was executed when the *Shaivas* still nearly all held the same doctrine. But to fix its age is a matter of some difficulty, and the only record that could have helped us to its solution—like too many other inscriptions that have been removed from their original sites by offici-

ous and dishonest pedantry—has long been lost. *Diogo de Couto*, the Portuguese annalist, says,—"When the Portuguese took Baçaim and its dependencies, they "went to this Pagoda and removed a famous stone over the entrance, that had "an inscription of large and well written characters, which was sent to the king, "after the Governor of India had in vain endeavoured to find out any Hindu or "Moor in the East who could decipher them. And the king D. Joáo III. also "used all his endeavours to the same purpose, but without any effect, and the "stone thus remained there—and now there is no trace of it."[25] Local tradition is too vague and varying to afford any hint at a probable date: one version is that, like most others all over the country, the *Pándavas*, when in banishment, excavated them in a single night; another, given by *De Couto*, says they were executed by a king of *Kánaḍá* named *Bánásura* who "ordered their construction, as "well as of some famous palaces near them, where he resided, of which even in my "time there were some vestiges and many ruins of cut stones and large unburnt "bricks. These palaces or the city, which is said to have been very beautiful, was "called *Sirbali*; and the hill where the pagoda of Elephanta is was called *Simpdeo*." But this *Báṇa*, the son of *Balí*, according to the later Purános at least, belongs to the age of *Kṛishna*, and though a devoted Shaiva who seems to have struggled desperately against the increase of Kṛishna-worship, his capital of *Shoṇita-pura* or *Devikota* in the *Karnátak* is too far off and his history too mythical to allow us to assign such works to him. The absurd tradition that they are the work of *Alexander the Great* is alluded to by Pyke in 1712, by Grose about 1751, and by Goldingham in 1795, and seems to find favour with the sergeants who of late have had charge of the cave.[26] Conjecture has been little less wild than tradition: the last cited writer would attribute them to a prince "who usurped the government in the 90th year of the Christian era, famed for his passion for architecture;" and Dr. Stevenson vaguely places their execution "some time between the eighth and twelfth centuries." Starting with the simple principle that architecture, like every other art, is progressive, though influenced by circumstances, Mr. Fergusson has developed criteria by which such works may be arranged as to relative age, and concludes that the great temple here, with the Dumar Leṇa at Elura, must have been executed in the tenth century of our era. There are certainly some grounds for this conclusion, which Dr. Wilson endeavours to support from historical probability[27]; yet while allowing that it may possibly date as late as the early half of the tenth century, the accordance of the sculptures at Elephanta with the pictures drawn by *Kálidása* in his *Kumára Sambhava* as early, probably, as the second half of the sixth century, and the differences in architectural details between what we find here and on remains of subsequent date, as well as the fact that an inscription such as the Portuguese carried off, if engraved in the characters of the tenth century, would still be legible to the Brahmans,—all tend to make me regard it as probably of the latter part of the eighth or of the ninth century of our era.

2. THE TRIMURTI.

P. 11.

I.—The Trimurti.

19. The most striking of the sculptures is the famous colossal three-faced bust, at the back of the cave, facing the entrance. This is called a Trimurti* or tri-form figure. It occupies a recess ten and a half feet deep—exclusive of the thickness of the pilasters in front which is about two and a half feet. The pilasters are fifteen and a half feet apart, but inside them the recess is 21 feet 6 inches in width; and the immense bust occupying it rises from a base about 2 feet 9 inches in height. In the corners of the opening, both in the floor and lintel, are holes as if to receive door posts, and in the floor is a groove, as if a screen had been used for occasionally concealing the sculpture or, perhaps there was a railing here to keep back the crowd.†

20. The *Trimurti* has been supposed by some to be an emblem of the Trinity,—but such an idea, in the Christian sense of the term, has perhaps no existence in the Hindu mind. Their triad is a creation not a manifestation of the divinity.[28]

21. There can be little doubt but that it represents *Shiva* as the supreme divinity of the pantheon: by what names we ought to call the three faces is however disputed. The notion connected with the common theory is that, though he is one god, yet as the world is supposed to be destroyed and renewed at the end of vast cycles of time, when a renewal is to take place the god causes to emanate from himself three forms to perform the functions of creation, preservation, and destruction. Now at Elura, where there are many figures of the sort, the central face appears to represent *Shiva* as the creator or generator; the left head—or that to the spectator's right, *Párvatí* or *Durgá*, his *shaktí* or female counterpart, and the third, *Rudra* or the destroying manifestation[29]. But at an early date we find the *Shaivas* calling the creator *Brahmá*—a divinity whom the Brahmans had invented as the god of prayer and the personification of their sect—and the preserver, *Viṣhṇu*, one of the inferior Vaidic gods, but latterly regarded by the Vaiṣhnavas as the supreme deity. *Kálidásá* asserts,—

> "In those three persons the one god was shown,
> Each first in place, each last,—not one alone;
> Of *Shiva*, *Vishnu*, *Brahmá*, each may be
> First, second, third, among the blessed three."[30]

The *Puránas* also appear to be rather suggestive of a triad of *Rudra*, *Viṣhṇu*, and *Brahmá*, than of one of *Rudra*, *Párvatí*, and *Shiva*; indeed all the Shaiva Puráṇas absorb the attributes of *Brahmá* and *Viṣhṇu* in their favourite divinity,[31] and but for the presence of what seem intended for certain feminine traits in the left face, we should be led unhesitatingly to infer, with Drs. Stevenson and J. Wilson, that the former one is here represented.

22. The central face—whether we call it a representation of *Shiva* as creator and generator, or of *Brahmá* who sprung from the left side of the supreme *Shiva* to

* From *tri* 'three,' and *murti* a 'figure,' or 'representation.' † See § 37.

create the world,[32]—has a mild and tranquil appearance; the lower lip is thick; the breast is ornamented with a necklace of large stones or pearls, and below it a deep elaborately wrought jewel breast ornament, the lower border of which is festooned perhaps with pearls; in the left hand he holds what may represent a pomegranate, a lotus-bud, or a gourd—as the *kamandala* or *patera*—the drinking vessel of an ascetic Brahman or *Yogi.* The right hand, like the nose, has been mutilated by some 'barbarian clothed in the garb of civilization,' but when it was entire, as represented in Niebuhr's drawing, it perhaps held the snake—the head of which still remains behind his right ear; and on the wrist is a thick ring like that still in use called *kadá.* The ears are divided and extended downwards like those of the *Kánphátás* —a set of *Yogis* or monks found in *Kachh,* who contrive to elongate the lobe of the ear to an extraordinary extent by means of weights.[33] In each ear he has a jewel with pendant ornaments—perhaps the ends of the lower necklace brought through the holes in the ear-lobes. The head-dress or *mukuta* is fastened, as we learn from comparison with other figures, by the folds or bands that encompass the neck: it is very richly wrought, representing doubtless such as was worn by princes in the age in which it was executed, and high up on the right side it bears a crescent—a peculiar emblem of *Shiva.* The jewel in front "is certainly," as Mr. Erskine remarks, "both for elegance of design and beauty of execution, one of the finest specimens of Hindu taste anywhere to be met with: some of the fancy-ornaments strongly resemble those used in heraldry. The hanging pendants have an elegant effect. The middle is occupied by a circular band of precious stones adorning and limiting the front; while below, another rich bandage, also adorned with cut stones, passes round the head-dress."[34]

23. The face to the spectator's left is that of *Rudra,* or *Shiva* the Destroyer, placed according to the Hindu rules for arranging images in temples, which direct that the principal face of *Shiva* must front the East. His right hand comes up before his breast, and—

> ————"fearful serpents twine,
> In scaly horror round that arm divine."

the *Cobra*—one of his favourite symbols, is twisted round the wrist, and with its hood expanded looks him in the face, while he appears to contemplate it with a grim smile. He has a large Roman nose and mustaches; his tongue appears between his slightly parted lips; and at the corner of the mouth a tusk projects downwards.[35] His eyebrows are not regularly arched, but somewhat twisted and slightly depressed towards the nose. The brow has an oval prominence in the centre, representing the third eye which *Shiva* has in his forehead, and from which the Brahmans say fire is to burst forth at the end of time to consume the world. This eye—called *Dnyanachakshu,* or 'the eye of knowledge,'—is always represented on his images, not in a horizontal position, but vertically as opening up the forehead; and as the whole temple was doubtless painted, there seems good reason for supposing that his third eye was depicted on the protuberance of the brow.

24. The *mukutas* or crowns on the side heads are not so high as that on the centre one. Among the ornaments on this one may be recognised some of the peculiar symbols of *Shiva*—a human skull over the left temple; a leaf of the *nirgundí;* a branch of the *bilva*—with its three leaves on each stalk like the trefoil; and high up a large cobra raises its expanded hood, whilst from under the cap, instead of hair, come twisted snakes. The back part of the ornament on the forehead has an unfinished appearance; and behind the *mukuta*, the stone is cut away into a shallow recess, dividing into two narrow slips, the one above the other, but without steps up to them. In these two persons might lie stretched at length without being seen from below.

25. The third face of the *Trimurti*—that to the spectator's right—has generally been regarded, and perhaps correctly, as *Shiva* in the character of *Vishnu*—the Preserver, holding in his right hand one of his emblems—a lotus flower. A comparison of this head, however, with that of *Párvatí* in some of the neighbouring sculptures elicits coincidences that render it not altogether improbable that it *may* be meant for the *shaktí* or wife of *Shiva:* the face has a gentle placid look, and is quite as feminine in character as that given to *Párvatí* in most of the other sculptures; the hair escapes in very neatly sculptured ringlets from under the head-dress, exactly as we find it on the female side of the *Arddhanári*, on the figure of *Párvatí* in the next compartment to the right, and everywhere else throughout the cave; and the *mukuta* bears a closer likeness to the feminine side of the *Arddhanári* head-dress than to that on any male figure among the sculptures. It is very elaborately and tastefully sculptured with festoons of pearl pendants; above the temple is a large leaf, probably that of the lotus; higher up, at the junction of the head with that of the central face, is carved the lotus flower *(padma);* and in front of it a small branch—perhaps a twig of the *Ashoka.* From the ear projects what was probably part of a large jewel, now broken off, but we again find something closely resembling it in the ear of the female side of the *Arddhanári.*

26. Such are the principal features of this remarkable sculpture of the triad *Shiva.*[36] Its total height is seventeen feet ten inches; a line drawn round the three heads at the level of the eyes measures twenty-two feet nine inches in length; and the distance between the wrists of the two side figures is twenty-two feet. The length of the middle face is four feet four inches,[37] of *Rudra's* face about five feet, and of the left face four feet one inch.

27. Every one must regret the thoughtless or mischievous wantonness of those visitors who, in 1865, broke off a portion of the noses of two of the faces of this bust, unique as it is in point of size and execution, and till then almost entire;[38] nor is this the last mutilation of the kind; about May 1868 the head of one of the leogriffs or tigers at the entrance of the eastern cave was broken off by some Europeans. It is very remarkable how prone certain classes of visitors are to destroy

the relics of ancient art, and this is so marked that, unless stopped by some means or other, the time will come when few of the more accessible antiquities of Western India will be worth visiting. Hector Macneil, who visited *Elephanta* about 1783, says—"It is difficult to write with any degree of temper on the dismal mutilations of this princely cavern, the stone of which is of such a durable nature as to have in a great measure baffled the ravages of time . . . and had it not been for the ingenuity of human madness, the caves of Elephanta would at this hour have been not only a valuable key to many inexplicable appearances in the other caves, but a noble monument of ancient architecture and sculpture. But what the hand of time has not been able to deface, the blind zeal of bigots and the childish tricks of fools have very nearly destroyed. . . . But what shall we say of those, who neither fired by bigotry, nor actuated by the rage of making proselytes, have wantonly displayed their ingenuity in lopping off heads, legs and arms from many of the most curious statues; and unable to do any more mischief by mutilation. . . wisely leaving their names behind them, as testimony of their profession, and the most satisfactory proofs of their stupidity and Gothic barbarism."[39] About 1849 a retired sergeant and guard of two native policemen were placed in charge of the caves, and the carving of names and other mutilations were for long prevented. Of late these foolish practices have been resumed, especially by nautical visitors, and followed up by Parsis and others. Whenever the sergeant attends to his duty, however, he can effectively stop such silly mischief.

28. On each side the Trimurti recess is a pilaster, in front of which stand gigantic guards or *dwárapálas*—door-keepers. The one to the right (at *a* on the Plan) is 12 feet 9 inches high, and is now the most entire of the two, though it appears to have suffered a good deal about the shoulders in comparatively recent times.[40] The cap, like most of those on the larger figures, is high, and has round it a sort of double coronal of plates, pointed above, the lower plates being smaller and the upper rising from within them. Between the lower ones on each side is a crescent with a star between its cusps, and behind the upper ones the cap presents the appearance of a deeply corrugated shell—a pattern finely developed on the central *mukuta* of the *Trimurti*, and which is probably intended to represent the rolls of twisted cloth in the turban. The plates around it bear such a resemblance to those still worn by the bridegroom in marriage processions among the Hindus in Western India as to suggest that ornaments of this sort were once in common use among their *Rájas.* The *dwárapála's* ears are large, and a pendant from the head-dress falls down behind the head. The left arm leans on the head of a *Pisháchu*, or dwarf demon,[41] and the fingers were clasped by those of the right hand.[42] Both arms had round bracelets or *kaḍá;* about the neck was a string of round beads; and a band passed over the left shoulder, down behind the hands and round the right hip, while a girdle bound his middle, and the ends of his robe hung down by the right side. The *Pisháchu* is about 7 feet high, and has on his head a wig with a smooth

surface; he wears a necklace, and a folded belt across his stomach. His right hand is raised to his breast; and the left, now broken off above the elbow, once hung down by his side.[43]

29. The *dwárapála* on the east side* is 13 feet 6 inches high, and is still more defaced than the other. In Niebuhr's time it seems only to have wanted part of the left arm and right leg with the left foot: now little remains except the head and shoulders.[44] The facets of the *mukuta* are broader than those on the other figure, and give a square appearance to the head-dress—every part of which is carved with great minuteness. In a circle on the upper facet or plate in front is a grotesque face *(kirtimukh)*; the lower is carved to represent a flower over jewels; and on each side of it is a flower, whilst the band that encircles the brow consists of three rows of pearls or jewels, from beneath which the hair crops out. The shell-like corrugations of the crown of the cap are beautifully executed, and from it there hangs down on the left side, a sort of long tassel reaching to the shoulder and formed apparently of several strands or curls of hair intertwisted;[45] on the right side is a fan-like frill representing the end of the turban cloth. In the ears are heavy rings like those called *kundala,* often represented in the ears of *Shiva* and other divinities, and worn by the religious mendicants called *gosávis,*—they differ from one another, and that on the left has a band passing over the ear to support it. The lips are thick, the face placid, and round the neck are the folds of a band going up behind the ear to the head-dress which it secures.[46] He wears a necklace of large round beads; a thick fillet falls as a festoon from his shoulders; and round the upper part of each arm he wears a bracelet (*báhu-bandha*) in the form of a snake twisted fully twice round—the ends being left free,—a form of ornament still in common use among Hindus. The right arm is bent just above the head of the attendant *Pishácha,* and the hand appears to have been open upwards in front of the side. Above the navel a string was knotted in front, and about the loins was a *kamarband,* with a *shela* or robe passing from the right hip over the left thigh and the ends dependent at the side. The *Pishácha* on his right was 6 feet 1 inch high, and the right leg of the *dwárapála* was advanced so far as to admit the arm of the *pishácha* behind it, so that his left hand and leg were seen between the legs of the *dwárapála.* His right hand was laid on his breast but is now broken away. His hair is tied in knots or knobs on the forehead and on each temple, with a fourth on the crown from which the hair hangs down. Across his shoulders a scarf passes, comes over the arm, and falls down on each side over his thighs. He has a band or, perhaps *langoti,* round the abdomen, ear-rings, bracelets, and a necklace to which a tortoise is attached as a pendant. He stands in a half crouching attitude, with prominent eyes, thick lips from between which his tongue has hung out, and with an odd smile he looks up to the *dwárapála.*

*** Marked *b* on the Plan.**

II.—The Linga Chapel.

30. In approaching the *Trimurti*, we pass the shrine or *garbha* of the temple on the right. It occupies an area equal to that enclosed by four columns ; and the architraves that connect the pillars to the east of it are cut off so as not to run into the walls of the shrine. It is entered by a door on each of the four sides, each approached by six steps (including the threshold), which raise the level of the floor of the sanctuary 3 feet 8 inches above that of the temple. On each side the doors is a gigantic *dwárapála* or guard, from 14 feet 10 inches to 15 feet 2 inches in height, and each standing on a low base.

31. From about the waist downwards many of these figures are almost entirely destroyed: that* on the east side of the south door, however, is entire. In the style of head-dress it differs from the other figures in the cave, except perhaps one or two of the *pisháchas*, and reminds one of an Egyptian statue. A large skull is carved above his forehead, the lips are parted to show the teeth, he has a single bead-necklace, ear-rings, plain twisted armlets, and thick *kaḍás* on his wrists. "He rests," says Dr. Hunter,[47] "on the right leg, and the knee of the left is a little bent. The right *humerus* hangs downwards, parallel to the body, and the forearm is bent in such a manner that the hand is opposite to the navel, the palm is turned upwards, and sustains a globe; and the fingers are bent a little backwards at their joining with the *metacarpus*, in a manner that admirably represents, or to speak more properly, makes the spectator almost feel, the weight of the body which they support." The left hand rests on the knot of the robe on the outside of his left thigh. "The left thigh and knee," continues Dr. Hunter, "are in particular well executed. The *patella* is distinctly formed, and you can clearly perceive the swelling of the *vasti* muscles, especially the *vastus internus*. The legs are not handsome as they taper from the knee, and have little or no calf; however, they much resemble those generally met with among the inhabitants of this country."

32. The *dwárapála* on the west side of the same door† is much mutilated, but the neck jewels, head-dress, and armlets have been very elaborately carved. That on the south side of the east door‡ is nearly entire except the face which is broken off: the turban is high in the crown; the plates round the head smaller than on most of the others; the ear-rings large; the end of the turban cloth formed into a circular frill behind the head, and the *janvi* or Brahmanical cord, which passes over his left shoulder and comes down to the upper part of his right thigh, consists of strands of beads or pearls twisted together. The end of the robe which hangs down by his left side is well executed. His fellow on the north side of the same door‖ has lost his legs and forearms and is damaged about the nose. It is a fine head. The band round the brow is richly carved, as are the large plates that rise

* Marked *c* on the Plan. † At *d*. ‡ At *e*. ‖ At *f* on the Plan.

3. THE LINGA CHAPEL.

P. 16.

from it and conceal the turban except the frilled end at the back. The hair falls down from under the cap to the shoulders in four series of neatly carved curls; the armlet *(keyúra)* on the left arm is broad, passing twice round, and jewelled at the ends and in the middle; the right forearm has been raised; and the *janvi* or sacred cord over the left shoulder is similar to that on the last *dwárapála*.

33. Passing to the north door, we have on its east side a similar figure,* but with the head-dress falling down on the left side in five thin folds overlapping one another. On the west side† the *dwárapála* is less defaced, and leans his left elbow on the head of a *pishácha* with bushy hair in small curls—perhaps intended to represent that of a negro. He has a ribbon tied round his waist, and a cobra comes over his right shoulder and rears its head in front. The *dwárapála* has a large circular ear-ring in the right, and a small one in the left ear; a thick mass, as of twisted cords, hangs down on the right side of the head from the top of the cap, and on the left side is the frill. On the cap are two crescents; behind the head a disc or shield; and beneath the usual bead necklace is a breast ornament; while the folds of his robe over the right hip and thigh are cleanly cut. Both *dwárapálas* on this side have had their right hands raised.

34. The figure on the south side of the west door‡ has a very elaborate head-dress secured by a folded tie round the neck; he has a crescent above each temple; a frill behind the head on the left side; and the top of the cap and the heavy roll that falls over on the right side are carved with open flowers and strands of cord or hair. The breast ornament, the *janvi* or sacred cord with its fastening on the left breast, and the broad jewelled waistband that held up the covering on the loins, have been wrought with much nicety. The lower part of the figure is quite gone. The companion *dwárapála*, on the north side,‖ is also entirely destroyed below, with the *pishácha* at his right side. He has a crescent over the right temple, and also on the left side of the head, and otherwise generally resembles the last, though the details are somewhat plainer. The style of sculpture of these statues is on the whole superior to that of many other figures in the cave. And from the character of most of the fractures we cannot suppose that they have been altogether so mutilated, as they now are, otherwise than wilfully.

35. The doors into the shrine have plain jambs with two plain fascias round them. Inside are the sockets of the door posts both in the floor and roof. The chamber or *sacellum* is perfectly plain inside, but like almost every other part of the cave the measurements of no two sides perfectly agree: the east side is 19 feet 4 inches, and the west 20 feet 2 inches, the north measures 19 feet 3 inches, and the south 18 feet 4 inches.[48] In the middle of the room stands a base or altar *(vedi)* 9 feet 9 inches square, moulded similarly to the bases under the *trimurti* and other sculptures, and about 3 feet high. In the centre of this is placed the *Liṅga*, cut from a stone of a harder and closer grain than that in which

* At *g* on the Plan. † At *h*. ‡ At *j*. ‖ At *k* on the Plan.

the cave is executed. The lower end of the *liṅga* is 2 feet 10 inches square, and is fitted into a hole in the *vedi* or base; the upper portion is circular, of the same diameter, about 3 feet in height, and rounded above. This plain stone, the mysterious symbol representative of *Shiva* as the male energy of production or source of the generative power in nature,—as the *Yoni* or circle in which it stands is of the passive or female power,[49]—is *the idol* of this temple, the central object of worship, to which everything else is only accessory or subsidiary. The *shaluṅka* or top of the pedestal is somewhat hollowed towards the *liṅga* to receive the oil, ghi, &c. poured on it by the worshippers, and which are carried off by a spout or *praṇáliká* on the north side, but this is now broken off.

36. As already mentioned, the *Shaiva* temples are generally attended by a *Gurava*, who alone can remove the stale flowers offered on the *Linga*, and who washes it before the daily worship commences. The ceremonies, as performed by the *Gurava* and by Bráhmaṇ differ somewhat, besides the *Gurava* omits the Sanskrit *mantras* which the Bráhman repeats at almost every stage of the ritual. The materials and instruments required for the complete daily *pujá* are as follows,—(1) a plate with fragrant flowers, *bilva* leaves, some fruit, a roll of *betel* leaves called *viḍá*—such as is eaten after meals, one or two copper coins, &c.; (2) a small vessel to hold *gandha*—a paste made of sandalwood sometimes mixed with saffron; *akshatá* or washed rice; *abira*—a fragrant powder made of sandalwood, zedoary, cypressus rotundus, &c.; (3) a large and a small water-vessel with a *pali*, ladle, or small cup, with which to pour the water; (4) a *shaṇkha* or conch shell on a tripod; (5) a bell; (6) a seat of wool or wood; (7) *abhiṣhékapátra*—a vessel with a hole in the bottom from which to drop water; (8) two lamps with wicks and *ghi* in them, and an *árti* or long shallow vessel with a piece of camphor to burn in it; (9) seven small cups containing milk, curds, *ghi* or clarified butter, honey, sugar, and sweetmeats; and (10) an *agarabatti* or *dhúpa*—a pastille or wick covered with aloe-wood powder, camphor, and other fragrant substances. The ministrant, provided with these requisites, seats himself in the shrine, and thrice takes a sip of water;[50] he then salutes *Gaṇapati*, the god and goddess of learning, the *Veda*, and other divinities; performs the *saṅkalpa*, that is, mentions the *tithi* or lunar date, the places of the planets, the place where he himself is, the object of his worship, &c.; and, that his worship may not be thwarted in any way, he calls on *Ganapati* by several of his names. He next purifies every part of his person and his seat by the repetition of *mantra* formularies, and then engages in *dnyana* or meditation. He now salutes the *Liṅga* and places *gandha*, *akshatá*, and flowers on the large water-vessel and on the conch, which is also filled with water; then he rings the bell that *Shiva* may attend and all sprites depart, and worships the *Liṅga* by placing *gandha*, rice, and flowers on it. The materials of worship and himself are next consecrated by sprinkling water from the shell upon them with a flower; and again he meditates. He is now ready to proceed with the first part of the

pujá. This he begins by invoking *Shiva*,[51] placing a seat or *ásana* for him, and offering to wash his feet with water;[52] then he pours over the *Liṅga* an oblation (*arghya*) of water mixed with *gandha*, *akshatá*, and flowers, and another—*áchamaniya*—that *Shiva* may cleanse his hands and mouth; next he washes or bathes the *Linga* with water, milk, curd, *ghi*, honey, and sugar;[53] again with water; then with water mixed with *gaṅdha*; and lastly with water. After wiping the idol with a cloth, he puts some grains of rice on it—this being symbolical of clothing an image; then he applies *gaṅdha*, rice, and flowers, repeating *mantras*, and swings round before it a lighted lamp and the *árti*, and at the same time rings the bell with his left hand; and offers *naivedya*, that is, raisins, sweetmeats, cocoanut, almonds, or plantains, adding *akshatá* to make up any deficiency. He concludes by asking *Shiva* to be satisfied with this part of the service and then removes the stale flowers from the top of the *Liṅga* to the north side of it. This part is often omitted: the second is more essential and is performed by the *Gurava* as well as the Bráhmaṇ. It is begun by holding the *abhishékápátra* over the *Liṅga* and allowing the water to drop through it upon the idol: this performance, called *snána*, lasting longer or shorter according to the *mantras* the worshipper chooses to repeat.[54] Wiping it with a clean cloth, he then applies rice for clothes (*vastra* and *upavastra*) as before, and a *yadnyopavíta*, then *gaṅdha*, or—dipping two fingers in the sandalwood paste—he draws them across the *Linga* so as to leave on the stone three curved streaks of paste from the edges of the fingers—thus forming the *tilaka* or sectarial mark on the front of it. Next he lays flowers and *bilva* leaves on the top of it, swings a lighted pastille (*dhúpa*) and lamp (*dípa*) before it, and at the same time rings the bell with his left hand. Then he offers *naivedya* or food before it, after which he sprinkles water with a flower on the *Linga*, that *Shiva* may wash his hands and mouth with it, and *gaṅdha* from a flower, that he may be freed from the smell of the food eaten. After this he offers fruit, *viḍa*—a roll of *betel* leaves with condiments,—and some small coins, and waves round it the lighted camphor. Next, keeping his right side towards it, he performs *pradakshiná* or goes round the *vedi* up to the *pranáliká* or spout, and then returns back, going round to it again —for he may not cross the water from the *pranáliká*; then he makes obeisance to the image with his *eight* limbs, that is, touches the ground with his forehead, breast, palms of the hands, knees, and toes; and, lastly, performing *mantra-pushpa* —placing some flowers on the idol, and confessing his ignorance and the deficiency of his worship, he concludes with further *mantras*. If he be a *Shudra*, he gives the offerings to the *pujári* or ministrant, who performs the worship for him. The *naivedya* placed before any divinity, except *Shiva*, may be removed and eaten by Bráhmans: in his case they are taken only by the *Guravas* or *Báwás*.

37. When this temple was in use, De Conto[55] tells us—the four gates of this shrine "were never opened except once in the year, on the day of its greatest

festivity, to show in what veneration they held the idol in question." It is probable, however, that he misunderstood his informants : it seems very improbable that the *linga* was shut up from any such feeling as he assigns ; and it is more likely that it was the great *Trimurti* that was ordinarily kept from vulgar gaze. At the *Shivarátri* festival the *linga* is still specially worshipped,—or rather the smaller one in the east wing of the cave,—and is frequently resorted to, as such objects often are among Hindus, by barren women, especially of the Baniyan caste.

III.—Arddhanáríshwara.

38. The compartment to the east of the *Trimurti*, (marked *A* on the Plan,) contains many figures grouped about a gigantic half-male, half-female, not unnaturally, mistaken by European visitors ignorant of Hindu mythology, for an Amazon ;[56]—such a being, however, as the Greeks fabled, is unknown to the Hindus. This represents *Shiva* as uniting in himself the personification of the two sexes, the union of *Shiva* and *Umá*,—and is call *Arddhanári* or *Arddhanáríshwara*.[57] Such a representation of the creative power must be of considerable antiquity, for exactly such a statue as this is mentioned by *Porphyry* as having been described to *Bardesanes* of Babylon by the Indian *Sandales* and his companions, ambassadors in the time of *Elagabalus*, about A.D. 220, and, what is curious, they described it as being of ten or twelve cubits in height, in a large cave in a mountain, standing erect, the right side being male from head to foot, the left female, and over the arms a number of angels,—particulars that could only refer to something very like what is actually found here.[58] This figure is (about eleven cubits) 16 feet 9 inches in height ; it leans to the right, which, as usual in the representations of *Arddhanári*, is the male side, and with one of its four arms rests on the bull *Nandi*—the vehicle of *Shiva*. An examination will show how carefully the distinction of the sexes is preserved in the two sides. The head-dress is the usual high one, with two heavy folds descending on the left or female side of it, and reaching the shoulder ; this bears a general resemblance to the *mukuta* on the left head of the *Trimurti*, while the right side differs in ornamentation and bears a crescent ;[59] on the left side the hair falls down along the brow in a series of neatly carved small ringlets, while on the right there is a line of knobs at the under edge of the cap. The right ear is lengthened downwards, and has only one ear-ring, but in the left are a *bali* or jewel in the upper part, and a large ring in the lobe. There is a slight protuberance on the forehead for the third eye of *Shiva*, and the girdle over the hips is tied at the left side where the ends hang down. The female breast and pelvis on the left are somewhat exaggerated. The male arms have both the twisted open armlets or *keyúra*, and on the wrists the *kadi* or thick rings—that on the front hand being knobbed as if set with jewels ; the left arms have broad armlets and a long solid bracelet

4. ARDDHANARISVARA.

P. 20.

(*kankaṇa*) with thick jewelled rings at the ends. The back pair of hands is in fair preservation, the right holds up the *nága* or cobra, a symbol of *Shiva*, and has a ring on the little finger; the left holds up a metallic mirror (*darshana*),[60] and has rings on the middle and little fingers. The front left hand hung downwards: it is now broken off, but seems, if Niebuhr's drawing is correct, to have held the lower portion of the robe of the goddess, part of which hangs over both her arms. The front right arm rests with the elbow on the hump and the hand on the left horn of the *Nandi*. The head of this holy bull, on which *Shiva* rides when he goes abroad, is in fair preservation, the length of the face is 2 feet 7 inches, and Dr. Wilson has remarked that in this instance it is not the domestic bull, as is now usually represented in connection with *Shiva*, but "the forest *Gava*, the *bos gavæus* of naturalists, mentioned in the *Veda* as an article of food."[61]

39. The lower portion of this compartment, which is about 16 feet wide, is much damaged, owing, it is alleged, to the rotting away of the rock by the water that lodges in the cave during the rains; but the preservation of the mouldings of the base below the figures, and the nature of some of the fractures indicate that more sudden and violent causes have also aided in the destruction. The figures on the right and left of the central one are generally connected with *Shiva* and *Párvatí* respectively: but in addition to the proper *gaṇa* or attendants of the two divinities, are some of the more notable members of the Pantheon. Opposite to the upturned back left arm, *Vishṇu* is represented riding upon *Gáruḍa*, who is his *váhana*. As in the usual representations of him, *Vishṇu* has here four arms; the front left hand seems to have rested on his knee, the other is raised and holds his *chakra* or discus, which is twirled about the forefinger put through the centre of it and thrown at the destined object; and they say when *Vishṇu* whirls it irresistible flames dart from its edge. Both the right hands are broken off—but perhaps one of them held the *shankha*—a large buccinum shell—one of his most usual symbols.[62] He sits on the shoulders of *Garuḍa* who holds him by the ankles. This *Garuḍa* or *Suparna*, the king of the feathered tribes, is a sort of half-eagle half-man, being generally represented with wings and a human face having a large hooked nose or beak; but in most places where he is figured throughout the cave his nose has been damaged—it is supposed by the Portuguese. In mythology *Garuḍa* is the son of *Kashyapa* and *Vinatá* and younger brother of *Aruha*—the legless charioteer of the Sun and the personification of Dawn; he is of incomparable swiftness and exquisitely beautiful plumage; his food was snakes, and, as he married *Shukí*, a very beautiful female, the serpent tribes, fearing lest his progeny might inherit his propensity for destroying them, waged a fierce war against him, but he destroyed them all except one, which he reserved as an ornament for his neck. This cobra is here represented with the head and tail knotted in front. From his enmity to the serpents, who were also the children of *Kashyapa* by his wife *Kadru*, *Garuḍa* was called *Nágantika*—serpent-destroyer. He is the wonderful bird of Hindu mythology, just as the Phœnix

was of the Greeks, the Simurgh of the Persians, the Anka or Rokh of the Arabs, the wise and ancient bird that sits on the ash Yggdrasil of the Edda, the Griffin of Chivalry, the Kirni of the Japanese and the sacred Dragon of the Chinese. As has long ago been remarked, *Garuḍa* here 'wears just such a wig as Sir Joshua Reynolds has given in his portrait of Dr. Johnson.'[63] On his forehead he has the *tilaka* or sectarial mark of the *Vaishṇavas*, and his large extended left wing may be clearly traced. Below this is a female bearing a fly-flap or *chaunri*—used to whisk off flies, usually made of the tuft on the tail of the Himálayan *Yák* or *Bos Grunniens*, and which among the Hindus, is regarded as a necessary emblem of royalty or exalted rank.[64] Her head-dress is carved with much minuteness of detail, a crescent is on the left side, and behind the head probably the *buchaḍá* or chignon bound about with flowers; she has large ear-rings and a triple necklace. Beside her are two dwarfs or *pisháchas*, and on her left is another female whose robe falls over her left arm and a sash or belt crosses the breast from each shoulder to the opposite hip—perhaps intended as the edges of a sort of *choli* or jacket. Her anklets (*núpura*) are thick like those in common use among Baniya women, and she carries on her left hand the dressing box of *Párvatí*, who is represented as somewhat fastidious about her toilette. Between *Garuḍa* and the central figure appears the bust of a female holding a flower in her left hand, above this the head of a *makara*—a heraldic-like monster emblematic of *Káma* the god of love, and two figures with wigs, one of which seems to ride on it. Behind *Vishṇu* are a male and a female figure with a dwarf below, the latter standing on a cloud and holding a *chámara*.

40. On the right or male side of *Arḍdhanári*, and on a level with *Vishṇu* and *Garuḍa*, are *Indra* and *Brahmá*. *Brahmá* is seated on a lotus throne (*padmásana*) which is supported by five wild geese (*hansa*) his chosen *váhana*. Three of his faces are visible, and the fourth usually given him may be supposed to be behind the central one. He has four hands,—the back right hand holds a lotus; the other now broken off was applied to his breast, as in Niebuhr's drawing and in other places in the cave; the outer left hand holds a *kamandala* or water-pot for his ablutions before prayer; and the inner one held a staff now destroyed. He is decked with ear-rings, two necklaces, bracelets, and a *shelá* or robe passing over his left shoulder and breast. The *Vedas* are now usually represented in his hands, and their absence in the representations of *Brahmá* in the cave has been considered as indicative of its having been executed before the modern *Pauranik* fictions about the eternity and divine authority of the *Vedas* had been concocted. In describing the eighth compartment we shall however have to allude to this again.

41. In a recess between *Brahmá* and the uplifted right arm of *Arddhanári* is *Indra*—the king of the *Vaidik* gods, the Jupiter Pluvius of the old Hindus, the god of the firmament—riding on the celestial elephant *Airavati*, who sends the rain from his trunk. The elephant's head is scarcely damaged. *Indra* holds the

5. SIVA AND PARVATI.

P. 23.

vájra or thunderbolt in his left hand and in his right what may have been the *ankúsh* or goad for driving the elephant.[65] Between *Indra* and *Brahmá* is a figure bearing two *chámaras* or *chaunris*, one in each hand. Below *Brahmá* is a large male figure with a high cap, holding the *trishula* or trident of *Shiva*, and doubtless intended for *Nandi* or *Nárada*, or some other personal attendant[66] of *Shiva's:* he has ear-rings differing on either side; a necklace; armlets like those on the other male figures; bracelets; a girdle; and the pendant from his cap hangs down in curls upon his left shoulder. Between this and the bull is a female with a *chámara* against her shoulder, and behind her is a dwarf and another female whose head has been destroyed.

42. In the upper portion of the compartment are thirteen figures, apparently *devangaṇa*—attendants of the gods.[67] Those to the spectator's left are evidently borne on clouds, and one of them has a dagger by his side; behind him is a female holding a round object in her left hand; and behind her is a *muni* or sage[68]—perhaps *Bhringi*—very lean, with a long beard, and an offering in his left hand; and lastly, behind him, is a small female figure mutilated. On the right is another *muni* with an offering in his hand and his hair curiously twisted into a *jathá* as it is worn by some religious ascetics; two figures over the head of *Arddhanári* hold garlands (half of one broken away) which just touch the head; and on the right are two larger male figures also holding garlands of celestial flowers.

IV.—Shiva and Párvatí.

43. The compartment to the west of the *Trimurti*, (marked *B* on the Plan,) is 13 feet wide by 17 feet 1 inch in height, with a base rising 2 feet 6 inches from the floor. The two principal figures are *Shiva*, and at his left hand his *shakti*—*Párvatí* or *Satí*. The relation of this sculpture to the last described is illustrated by the following quotation from the *Linga Purána*:—" *Daksha* having produced his mental daughter *Satí*, adapted for *Shiva*, applied her to the lord *Rudra*. At the beginning of the multiplication of creatures (*Brahmá*) sprung from the golden egg said to this *Ardhanáríshwara*:—' Divide thyself' then she sprang forth a fair female, and, as portions of her, all the females in the three worlds have been produced in succession; and from the male sprang, as portions of him, the eleven *Rudras*, &c. She was entirely a female and he entirely a male." *Kálidása* thus expresses the same idea,—

> " Thou, when a longing seized thee to create,
> Thy single form in twain didst separate;
> The Sire, the Mother, that made all things be
> By their first union were but parts of thee,
> From them the life that fills this earthly frame,
> And fruitful Nature self-renewing came."[69]

44. The figure of *Shiva* is 16 feet high, and has four arms,—the two left ones now broken off. As elsewhere, he has a high cap with three pointed plates rising out of the band of it, and a smaller one in front of that on the forehead. Between these is a crescent over each temple. From the crown rises a sort of cup or shell in which is a singular three-headed female figure of which the arms are broken off. The *Gangá* or Ganges is fabled to flow from *Shiva's* hair, and the three heads probably represent the three principal streams which, according to Hindu geography, form the main stream of their sacred river, namely the *Gangá*, the *Yamuná* or Jamná, and the *Saraswatí* which they suppose unite at *Práyag* or Allahabad,—the junction being called *Triveni* or the "three plaited locks," one of the most sacred places of Hindu pilgrimage. This bust is a female triad, the mythological union of the *shaktis* or consorts of the three great divinities: *Gangá*, the daughter of *Himálaya* is *Umá* or *Párvatí* and would be represented as of white complexion; *Lakshmí*, the consort of *Vishṇu*, as *Yamuná* is blue; and *Saraswatí* the spouse of *Brahmá*, on *Umá's* right, would be red.[70] *Shiva* wears a necklace, the usual open armlets, heavy bracelets, and ear-rings. An ornamented girdle binds his waist, from under which his garment comes down, is brought round the right side, and tied in a knot outside the left thigh. Over his left shoulder a *yadnyopavíta* or sacred cord hangs down in front of his right side and passes over his right arms. The back right hand holds a snake, the tail hanging down upon the arm, while the body passes behind his back, and the cobra's expanded hood is raised outside his left shoulder. The front right hand is raised as if to command attention, but it is damaged. The back left hand appears to have passed over *Párvatí's* breast, and with one of the fingers to have touched her under the chin; but it is broken off above the wrist; the other has been broken off comparatively recently:—it rested on the head of a *Pishácha*, who seems to stagger under its weight. This dwarf has a dense wig of curly or plaited hair, held a *chámara* in his left hand and a small cobra in his right, has a tortoise suspended at his necklace, and wears a waist-belt and *langoti*.

45. It may be remarked once for all, that it seems to have been a conventional custom among Indian sculptors, when representing clothed figures, to overlook all minor details of drapery, and at most to carve only those portions of the garments where they are gathered into thick folds and the outer hems of them. The effect of this, combined with the scantiness of the clothing for the upper part of the body before the Muhammadan conquest of India, is to give most of the figures an appearance of nudity which close inspection shows was not intended. In most instances where the figures are perfect in this cave, we find on the thighs, legs, or ankles, and often very delicately carved—the hem of a garment which comes down from the tie about the waist. We have this very distinctly indicated in the case of the figure of *Párvatí* in the compartment under notice. The shoulders and breast seem to have been generally left bare, when indoors at least, but were probably covered by the *shelá* when outside.[71]

46. On *Shiva's* left stands *Párvatí*, about 12 feet 4 inches high, wearing a circlet round the brow from under which the hair is represented in small curls round the brow. The head-dress rises in tiers, and has a pointed plate in front, and behind the neck on the right side is a sort of cushion—perhaps of the back hair. She wears heavy ear-rings—the one unlike the other, several necklaces, broad armlets and bracelets, with a girdle having an ornamented clasp, and heavy anklets. Her dress comes over the right leg, the corner falling to the ankle and then passing over the left leg, and a loose robe hangs over her right arm. With her right hand she seems to touch the *chámara* of the *Pishácha*, or perhaps she leans on his shoulder; and her left hand is over the head of a female dwarf with very large elliptical ear-rings, a huge chignon, and richly carved armlets, dressed with a garment of which the corner falls down in front, and carrying by cords or straps a bundle or box over her left shoulder. This sculpture may be regarded as the representation of *Shiva* and *Párvatí* as the progenitors of the human race, or indeed of all animal life.

47. On *Shiva's* right, as in the last compartment, are *Brahmá* and *Indrá*. *Brahmá* has four hands, one of the right holding a lotus, the other applied to his breast, and the left hands appear to have held a rod and perhaps his *patera* or water vessel. He is mounted on his lotus seat carried by five geese. Close to his left is *Indra* on his elephant, holding up his left hand towards *Shiva*. On *Párvatí's* left we find *Vishṇu* on *Garuḍa*, his back right hand holding a mace or club, the front one broken off, his front left hand rests on his knee, and the other holds his *chakra*. He wears armlets and a necklace, and his feet rest in *Garuḍa's* hands as stirrups. In this place *Garuḍa* has wig-like hair but no mustaches or *tilaka*, and his face is scarcely damaged. He wears the *Nága* knotted round his neck. The figures below *Brahmá* on *Shiva's* right are much defaced. Next to him, and in front, is a male kneeling on his right knee with his arms crossed on his breast and a dagger or knife on his right side. Round his head is a band with a large rosette or frill behind, like what we have already noticed in describing the *Dwárapálas* of the shrine; and from under the band the hair falls in three lines of ringlets reaching to his shoulders. Though small, this is probably a character of some importance: can it be *Káma*, the Indian Cupid, who plays so prominent a part in *Kálidása's* poem? Behind him stands a female *chámara*-bearer, with anklets, wristlets, and holding a flower in her left hand raised towards her cheek. Behind her is a taller female with broad armlets and thick anklets, but whose hands and face are broken; and at the back of this again and above the *chámara*-bearer is the head of a figure with curly hair, and holding in the left hand what may perhaps have been an offering. The rest is destroyed.

48. Above *Brahmá* are clouds on which are six figures,—the largest a male with high head-dress and double necklace, holding a long packet[72] wrought all over the surface with flowers divided by narrow fillets or ribbons round it. Immediately before and behind him are female figures; nearer *Shiva's* head are

two males—one of them a bearded *Muni;* and behind the rest is another male with a moustache. Above *Párvatí* also are six figures, similarly disposed, and all flying or floating on clouds,—the female behind the larger figure having a head-dress like a Turkish turban and a richly carved belt.

V.—Marriage of Shiva and Umá.

49. Passing by the south side of the shrine to the west porch, we come to the fourth compartment (marked C in the Plan), which *De Couto* says had "a beautiful porch of mosaic workmanship." It represents the marriage of *Shiva* and *Párvatí,* in which she stands at his right hand,—a position which the wife rarely occupies except on the day of her marriage.[73]

50. The legend of the marriage is well told by *Kálidása.* After the death of *Satí*, his first consort, *Shiva* is represented as practising austerity—the only certain means by which a Hindu, whether god or man, can attain unbounded power, when *Umá*, (who is *Satí* in another birth,) became enamoured of him, and by penance secured his affection. He then sends the Seven Sages[74] to ask his daughter of *Himálaya*, who meets them with a gift:—

> "Earth to her centre shaking at his tread;
> By his dark lips with mountain metals dyed,
> His arms like pines that clothe his lofty side—
> By his proud stature, by his stony breast,
> Lord of the Snowy Hills he stood confest."

They arrange the fourth for the marriage day, and the following extracts from the seventh *Sarga* or Canto of the *Kumára Sambhava*,[75] is the best account of the nuptials and their accompaniments:—

> "In light and glory dawned the expected day
> Blest with a kindly star's auspicious ray,
> When gaily gathered at *Himálaya's* call
> His kinsmen to the solemn festival.
> * * * * *
> And she, their child, upon her bridal day
> Bears her dear parents' every thought away—
> * * * *
> Each noble matron of *Himálaya's* race
> Folds his dear *Umá* in a long embrace,
> Pours blessings on her head, and prays her take
> Some priceless jewel for her friendship's sake—
> * * * * *
> Then to a court with canopies o'erhead
> A crowd of noble dames the maiden led—
> A court for solemn rites, where gems and gold
> Adorn the pillars that the roof uphold.
> * * * *

6. MARRIAGE OF SIVA AND UMA.

P. 26.

Through her long tresses one a flower-wreath wound,
And one with fragrant grass her temples crowned,
While o'er her head sweet clouds of incense rolled
To dry and perfume every shining fold.
Bright dyes of saffron and the scented wood
Adorned her beauty, till the maiden stood
Fairer than *Gangá* where the Love-birds play
O'er sandy islets in her silvery bay.

* * * *

The happy mother took the golden dye
And raised to hers young *Umá's* beaming eye—
Then swelled her bosom with maternal pride
As thus she decked her darling for a bride—
Oh, she had longed to trace on that fair brow
The nuptial line, yet scarce could mark it now!
On *Umá's* rounded arm the woollen band
Was fixt securely by the Nurse's hand—
Blind with the tears that filled her swimming eye,
In vain the mother strove that band to tie.
Spotless as curling foamflakes stood she there,
As yielding soft, as graceful and as fair—
Or like the glory of an autumn night,
Robed by the full moon in a veil of light.
Then at her mother's hest, the maid adored
The spirit of each high ancestral lord,
Nor failed she next the noble dames to greet,
And give due honour to their reverend feet."

The dress and progress of *Shiva* are next described in these terms:—

"His own dire vesture took a shape as fair
As gentle bridegroom e'er could wish to wear—
The withering skull that glazed the eye with dread,
Shone a bright coronal to grace his head;
That Elephant's hide the god had worn of old
Was now a silken robe inwrought with gold;
Ere this his body was with dust besprent,
Soft unguent now it shed delightful scent;
And that mid-eye which, glittering like a star
Shot the wild terror of its glance afar—
So softly now its golden radiance beamed—
A mark of glory on his forehead seemed.
His twining serpents, destined still to be
The pride and honour of the deity,
Changed but their bodies—in each sparkling crest
The blazing gems still shone their loveliest.
What need of jewels on the brow of him
Who wears the crescent Moon?—no spot may dim
Its youthful beauty, e'en in light of day
Shedding the glory of its quenchless ray.

Well-pleased the god in all his pride arrayed
Saw his bright image mirrored in the blade
Of the huge sword they brought ; then calmly leant
On *Nandi's* arm, and toward his Bull he went,—
Whose broad back covered with a tiger's hide,
Was steep to climb as mount *Kailása's* side,
Yet the dread monster humbly shrank for fear
And bowed in reverence as his lord drew near.
The matrons followed him, a saintly throng,
Their earrings waving as they dashed along—
Sweet faces, with such glories round them shed
As made the air one lovely lotus bed.
On flew those bright ones—*Káli* came behind,
The skulls that decked her rattling in the wind :
Like the dark rack that scuds across the sky,
With herald lightening and the crane's shrill cry.

* * * * *

* The *Sun* presents a silken shade
Which Heaven's own artist for the god had made,
Gilding his brows, as though bright *Gangá* rolled
Adown his holy head her waves of gold.
She in her goddess-shape divinely fair,
And *Yamuná* sweet River-nymph, were there,
Fanning their lord, that fancy still might deem
Swans waved their pinions round each Lady of the Stream.
E'en *Brahmá* came—Creator—Lord of might,—
And *Vishṇu* glowing from the realms of light.

* * * * *

By *Indra* led, each world-upholding lord
With folded arms the mighty god adored,—
In humble robes arrayed, the pomp and pride
Of glorious deity were laid aside ;
They signed to *Nandi*, and the favourite's hand
Guided his eye upon the suppliant band.

* * * * *

He moves to go ; from his moon-crest a ray
Sheds quenchless light on his triumphant way.
On through the air his swift Bull bore him well
Decked with the gold of many a tinkling bell,
Tossing from time to time his head on high,
Enwreathed with clouds as he flew racing by,
As though in furious charge he had uptorn
A bank of clay upon his mighty horn."

As he approaches the capital of *Himálaya*—

" Forth from the gates a noble army poured
To do meet honour to the mighty lord ;
With all his friends on elephants of state
The King of Mountains passed the city gate,
So gaily decked, the princes all were seen
Like moving hills inwrapt in bowery green,

As the full rushing of two streams that pour
Beneath one bridge with loud tumultuous roar,
So through the city's open gate streamed in
Mountains and gods with tumult and with din.

* * * * *

Onward in peerless glory *Shiva* passed,
Gay banners o'er his way their shadows cast,—

* * * * *

Through the broad streets with loud acclaim he rode
And reached the palace where the king abode;
As leaves the sun a cloud at eventide,
There he descended from his monster's side.
Leaning on *Vishnu's* arm he passed the door
Where mighty *Brahmá* entered in before;
Next *Indra* came, and all the Host of Heaven,
The noble saints and those great Sages seven;
Then led they *Shiva* to a royal seat,
Fair gifts they brought, for such a bridegroom meet,
With all due rites, the honey and the milk,
Rich gems were offered and two robes of silk.

At length by skilful chamberlains arrayed
They led the lover to the royal maid.

* * * *

He gazed on *Umá*;—from his lotus eyes
Flashed out the rapture of his proud surprise,
Then calm the current of his spirit lay
Like the world basking in an autumn day
They met; and true love's momentary shame
O'er the blest bridegroom and his darling came;
Eye looked to eye—but quivering as they met,
Scarce dared to trust the rapturous gazing yet.
In the god's hand the priest has duly laid
The radiant fingers of the Mountain-Maid,
Bright as if Love with his dear sprays of red
Had sought that refuge in his hour of dread."

51. The meeting of the bridal pair is probably the scene intended in this sculpture—unfortunately very much damaged now. *Shiva* is 10 feet 10 inches high, but of his four hands only the front left one remains entire, and the whole of his right leg is gone. He wears the usual high *mukuta* or cap with the corrugated crown, and has behind it a sort of oval disc occupying the place of the nimbus or aureole depicted round the heads of emperors and demigods by the old western nations, and behind the head of *Buddha* in the paintings and sculptures of the caves of his sect in Western India. He has a girdle about his waist, and his robe comes over his right hip and is knotted at his left side—his hand resting on the knot, while the ends hang loosely down. His *yadnyopavita* or sacred cord hangs down from his left shoulder, passes down to his right thigh and over his right arms.

52. *Párvati* or *Umá* is 8 feet 6 inches high, her head-dress is lower than in the

last compartment; the hair escapes in little curls from under the broad jewelled fillet that binds the brow; and behind the head is a small disc—possibly in this case a part of the dress. She wears heavy ear-rings, and several necklaces, from one of which a string hangs down between her breasts and ends in a tassel. The robe that hangs from her zone is indicated by a series of slight depressions between the thighs. She slightly inclines her head, as if bashful, and is being pushed forward by a large male figure—possibly her father *Himálaya*—who lays his right hand on her right shoulder while his left hand holds up a necklace of beads near her left ear. Both her hands are broken off, but probably the left was laid in *Shiva's* right, as it is in a similar sculpture at *Elura*. This figure appears to have been one of the best proportioned and most carefully executed in the cave. The high cap and so much of the dress of the male figure behind her as is visible have also been carved with more than usual minuteness.

53. At *Shiva's* left, crouching on his hams, is a three-faced figure, much defaced, that Erskine thought might probably be *Kártikeya*, the War-god and son of *Shiva* and *Umá*; but which is doubtless *Brahma*, who is represented as acting the part of priest in the ceremony: "Then," says the *Linga Puráṇa*, bowing "reverentially, and rejoicing in spirit, the great father of *Brahmaloka*, the supreme "lord, joined the hands of the god and goddess,"[76] *Kálidása* thus continues his description of the rites :—

"Around the fire in solemn rite they trod—
The lovely lady and the glorious god;
Like Day and starry Midnight when they meet
In the broad plains at lofty *Meru's* feet.
Thrice at the bidding of the priest they came
With swimming eyes around the holy flame;
Then at his word the Bride in order due
Into the blazing fire the parched grain threw,
And toward her face the scented smoke she drew,
While softly, wreathing o'er her cheek it hung,
And round her ears in flower-like beauty hung.

* * * * *

'This flame be witness of your wedded life,—
Be just thou Husband, and be true, thou Wife!'
Such was the priestly blessing on the Bride,—
Eager she listened, as the earth when dried
By parching summer suns drinks deeply in
The first soft droppings when the rains begin.

'Look, gentle *Umá*,' cried her lord, 'afar
Seest thou the brightness of yon polar star?
Like that unchanging ray thy faith must shine!'
Sobbing, she whispered, 'Yes, for ever thine!'

The rite is o'er—her joyful parents now
At *Brahma's* feet in duteous reverence bow:

7. SIVA AND PARVATI IN KAILASA.

P. 31.

> Then to fair *Umá* spake the gracious Power
> Who sits enthroned upon the Lotus flower :—
> 'O beautiful lady, happy shalt thou be,
> And hero children shall be born of thee !' "[77]

54. Behind stands either *Vishṇu* or *Surya*, with four hands and a peculiar cylindrical cap from under which his hair appears in abundant curls. In his front right hand he holds a lotus and in the back left hand the *chakra*; the other two are broken off. On the extreme right stands a female who may be *Mená*, the mother of *Umá*, while the female figure over *Umá's* head with a *chámara* is perhaps *Saraswatí*, who appears at the marriage, and at the conclusion of the ceremony is thus introduced :—

> " In two-fold language on each glorious head
> The Queen of Speech her richest blessings shed ;
> In strong, pure, god-like utterance for his ear,
> To her in liquid tones, soft, beautifully clear."[78]

55. On *Párvatí's* right stands a female *chámara* bearer with necklaces, pendent ear-rings, and holding part of her robe in her left hand. Behind her is a larger male figure with a plain cap, hair curled like a barrister's wig, and a large crescent behind his neck identifying him as *Chandra*, the Moon-god, bearing a large round pot of water for the marriage ceremony. Above *Shiva's* head are—first, a male between two females, the heads of all of which are damaged, and then above them two smaller figures. On the other side are six more figures,—a male and two females below, and above two bearded *Munis* or *Rishis*, and *Bhringi* next to *Shiva's* head, with a small figure on the roof.

VI.—Shiva and Párvatí in Kailása.

56. Following the order proposed by Stevenson, the fifth compartment to be described is that (marked *D* on the Plan) on the south side of the eastern portico. It is sadly defaced now, though in Niebuhr's time the faces of nine of the lower figures seem to have been entire. *Shiva* and *Párvatí* are represented in it seated together on a raised floor and both adorned as in the other sculptures. *Shiva* had four arms, all of them now broken, and a disc or nimbus behind the head, but the whole face with the cap is split off. He has had armlets of the usual spiral form with open ends, his *janvi* lies across his shoulders, and part of his robe comes over his knees. *Párvatí* is seated at his left hand, and wears the same pendent tassel hanging down between her breasts from a thick twisted necklace as in the last described group. Over the left arm and on the right thigh and leg portions of her garments may still be traced. Behind her right shoulder stands a female figure carrying a child astraddle on her left side as they usually are carried in India: this is probably intended to represent a nurse bearing *Kártikeya*, called also *Skanda* and *Mahásena* the War-god,[79] the son of *Shiva*, born to destroy the power of *Tárak*,

a giant demon, who by penance secured such power that he troubled earth, hell, and heaven, and—

"Like some dire comet, gleaming wild affright,"

deprived the gods of their sacrifices, and drove them in pitiable fright to seek the aid of *Brahmá*, who thus answered them :—

"'Tis not for me, my children, to create
A chief to save you from your mournful fate ;
Not by my hand the Fiend must be destroyed,
For my kind favour has he once enjoyed,
And well ye know that e'en a poisonous tree
By him who planted it unharmed should be ;
He sought it eagerly, and long ago
I gave my favour to your demon-foe,
And stayed his awful penance, that had hurled
Flames, death, and ruin o'er the subject world.
When that great warrior battles for his life,
O, who may conquer in the deadly strife,
Save one of *Shiva's* seed ! He is the Light,
Reigning supreme beyond the depths of night."

He then suggests the marriage of *Shiva* and *Umá*, adding that—

"— from their love a mighty child shall rise,
And lead to war the armies of the skies ;
Freed by his hand, no more the heavenly Maids
Shall twine their glittering hair in mournful braids."[80]

57. This child, Erskine supposes to be that represented in this sculpture; Stevenson, on the other hand, regards it as "*Vináyaka* or *Gaṇesha* usually in Bombay called *Gaṇapati*, *Shiva's* eldest son," and assigns as his reason for this that "the account of production of *Vináyaka* or *Gaṇesha*" immediately follows the legend of the marriage in the *Liṅga Puráṇa*, and that "he afterwards acts a more important part, and much more is said about him than about his brother, who is not mentioned till afterwards."[81] But if the later *Puráṇas* give more prominence to the god of prudence, the older *Kumára Sambhava* is exclusively devoted to the origin of the War-god.

58. On *Párvatí's* left stands a female attendant and, farther off, a larger male figure who seemingly held his right-hand to his breast and rested his left on the knot of his robe at his side. Behind *Shiva's* right shoulder is another female with a *chámara*, and at his feet his faithful attendant and worshipper *Bhringi*,[82] emaciated almost to a skeleton, and now deprived of his head, while behind him stands a tall figure, with the usual high head-dress, ear-rings, necklace, and robe covering his left arm down to the wrist, and passing under his right. At his foot, in a recess behind the pilaster, stands a small dwarf 3 feet in height, with his arms crossed.

59. Beneath, or in front of the platform on which the principal figures rest, the sculpture is so defaced that little can now be made out satisfactorily. Directly

8. RAVANA UNDER KAILASA.

P. 33.

under *Párvati* is the bull *Nandi*, and at his left shoulder a face with a wig such as is elsewhere given to *Garuḍa*. Below him are two animal figures, possibly monkeys, though Erskine thinks the lower one was the tiger the *váhana* of *Párvati*, which, he says, the *pishácha* behind holds by the left hind leg: this is very doubtful. Whether *Brahmá* and *Indra* figured in the left side, or how it was filled up, cannot now be determined. The rock over the heads of *Shiva* and *Párvati* is carved into patterns somewhat resembling irregular frets disposed on an uneven surface—perhaps intended for the rocks of *Kailása*.[83] On clouds on each side are the usual celestial attendants, perhaps *Gandharvas* and *Apsaras* rejoicing and scattering flowers. Some of the male figures have curly wigs, and on each side is a skeleton-like *Ṛishi*, one of whom has a basket in his left hand while he scatters flowers with his right. On the roof is the body of a small fat figure, which Erskine supposes may be meant for *Gaṇesha*—the second son of *Shiva* and *Párvati*, who was born, say the latter Hindu legends, with a human head, but lost it.

VII.—Rávaṇa under Kailása.

60. On the north side of the eastern portico is a compartment facing the last and similar to it (marked *E* on the Plan), in which *Shiva* and *Párvati* again appear seated together in the upper half of the recess. The protuberance or third eye of *Shiva* is distinctly marked, his cap is elegantly carved with a disc behind it and bears the crescent, and he has large pendent ear-rings. He had eight arms, all more or less broken now; two of them rested on the head of attendants, and in one of the back right hands he held the *trishula* or trident—the head of which still remains. On his right sat *Párvati*, but little except her trunk is left. On each side of the compartment is also a large figure somewhat like the *dwárapálas* around the shrine, but with a protuberance on the brow, and that to the spectator's right having a skull prominently carved on the forehead and snakes coming round from behind his left shoulder. "The *Shiva Gita*," says Erskine, "distinguishes four classes of worshippers who have been accepted of the god; one of these possesses *swarupta* or similarity of appearance. 'He who worships me disinterestedly,' says the deity, 'by knowing me gains my form, and lives in my dominions.'" The same protuberance is met with on the forehead of servants of *Shiva* in other compartments at Elephanta.[84] To the left of *Shiva* are several figures all more or less defaced: on the head of one of them he leans his hand, and in front near his foot is *Bhringi*, easily distinguished by his skeleton ribs. On *Bhringi's* left, and in front of the large figure behind the pilaster, is *Gaṇesha* or *Gaṇapati* with his elephant head. That there was any appropriateness in giving to the god of Prudence and Wisdom the head of the most sagacious of animals, does not seem to have occurred to the writers of the *Puráṇas*, and they have accordingly invented more

than one silly legend to account for his figure. One of them says that upon a time *Gaṇesha*, having quarrelled with *Vishṇu*, was likely to have gained the victory when *Shiva* interposed and cut off his head, but his mother *Párvatí* in anger at this began austerities that threatened to upset the whole celestial polity—for against austerities and sacrifices performed in strict ritualistic form even the gods are powerless,—and in dismay they assembled to beseech *Shiva* to stop his consort by the restoration of her son. But even gods are sometimes at a loss,—*Gaṇesha's* head could nowhere be found, and in their haste it was determined to replace it by that of the first animal that could be met with: this happened to be an elephant with one tusk; further to appease *Párvatí*, who had formed him from the scurf scraped from her body in bathing, *Shiva* agreed to adopt him as his son; and the other gods consented that on all occasions he should be first invoked. Hence, all inscriptions and the like begin by a formula of invocation to *Gaṇapati*. Another account says when all the gods were summoned to see the infant *deva*, *Shaní* or Saturn, knowing the baneful effect of his glance, refused to look at the child, till *Párvatí*, taking it as an insult that he should not admire her son, provoked him to cast his eyes on *Gaṇesha* whereby his head was reduced to ashes.

61. While *Shiva* and his attendants are thus represented seated in *Kailása*, under it is the tenfaced *Ravaṇa*, king of *Lanká* or Ceylon, the grandson of *Pulastya*, the son of *Brahmá*. According to the legend, *Rávaṇa* got under the silver mountain that he might carry it to *Lanká*, and so have *Shiva* all to himself and make sure of his aid against *Ráma*. *Párvatí* perceiving the movement called to *Shiva*—"Some one moves the hill, we shall be overthrown," on which *Shiva* raising his foot pressed down the mount on *Rávaṇa's* head, and fixed him where he was for ten thousand years, until his grandfather *Pulastya* taught him to propitiate *Shiva* and perform austerities, after which he was released, and, notwithstanding all his crimes, became a devoted *Shaiva*. The attitude of *Shiva*, as remarked by Erskine, "while he rests his hands on the heads of his two servants, is not unlike the position of one who steadies himself on being sensible of sudden motion." *Rávana's* back is turned to the spectator, and a sword is stuck in his waist-band, his faces are entirely obliterated, and only a few of his twenty arms are now traceable. Beside him there were perhaps some *Pisháchas* as at *Elura*. Above *Shiva* are numerous figures—one almost a skeleton; and on his left is *Vishṇu* on *Garuḍa*, while in a recess is the tiger of *Párvatí* couched on his paws. Sculptures similar to this are also found at *Jogeshwari* in *Salsette* and at *Elura* or *Verula*, but at the latter place the arrangements differ somewhat from those of this sculpture. "*Rávaṇa*, I suppose," says Stevenson, "to be the type of the rude aborigines who inhabited India before the Brahmans and high caste Hindus from the north invaded the country. The moral taught in this compartment, then, is *Shiva's* power over these rude aborigines, and their devotion to his worship."[85]

9. BHAIRAVA OR KAPALABHRIT.

P. 35

VIII.—Bhairava, Mahákála, or Kapálabhrit.

62. Passing again to the west end of the cave, we find a compartment on the north side of the portico and facing the marriage of *Shiva* (marked *F* on the Plan), containing one of the most remarkable sculptures in the cave. It is much damaged below, but we have it again both at *Elura* and *Amboli*. The principal figure has been a standing one about eleven and a half feet in height, but the left foot has been raised on some step or higher level than the right. The head-dress is high and has much carving upon it, with a skull and cobra over the forehead and the crescent high up on the right. The face is indicative of rage, the lips set, with tusks projecting downwards from the corners of the mouth, and the eyes large as if swollen. Over the left shoulder and across the thighs hangs the *ruṇdamálá* or rosary of human skulls.[86] A weapon seems to have been stuck into the waist-cloth, of which some folds hang over the right hip. His arms were eight, but five of them with both the legs are now broken,—the front right and left hands were destroyed by the Portuguese in the sixteenth century, and the others have suffered since. All the arms have broad ornaments under the shoulders, and bracelets on the wrists. It does not now appear how the small human body on his left was supported, but at *Elura* it is transfixed by a short spear held in the front left hand, and the same was probably the case here :—it has now lost the head, both arms, and one of the legs, and the other rests on a sort of projecting ledge of the rock. The second right hand wields a long sword, without guard, with which he seems about to slay his victim; the third left hand holds a bell as if to intimate the moment to strike the fatal blow; and the second presents a bowl under the victim as if to receive its blood, while a cobra twists round the arm. The third right hand, according to De Couto and Niebuhr's drawing, held up a human form by the legs, as in the corresponding figure at *Elura*.[87] The fourth left arm has been broken since Erskine's time, but, with the corresponding right hand, it supported a screen that forms a sort of background or panel for the principal figure, at the side of which is the head of an elephant, whence we may suppose it is intended to represent the *Gajacharma* or elephant's hide, which he wraps round his loins, but which, in the state of frenzied excitement in which he is here represented, he flourishes in the air.

> " The Elephant hide that robes thee, to thy steps
> Swings to and fro ;—the whirling talons rend
> The crescent on thy brow ;—from the torn orb
> The trickling nectar falls, and every skull
> That gems thy necklace laughs with horrid life.
> Attendant spirits tremble and applaud ;
> The mountain falls beneath the powerful arms,
> Around whose length the sable serpents twine
> Their swelling forms, and knit terrific bands,
> While from the hood expanded frequent flash
> Envenomed flames.

As rolls thy awful head,
The low'ring eye that glows amidst thy brow
A fiery circle designates, that wraps
The spheres within its terrible circumference."[88]

63. This sculpture has been usually interpreted as *Vírabhadra*, one of the *avatáras* of *Shiva*, created to destroy the sacrifice of *Daksha*. The legend is told in many forms, but in the *Mahábhárata*[89] it runs thus :—*Daksha* began a sacrifice to *Vishṇu* at *Gangádwára* in the *Himálaya*, which was attended by various orders of divine beings including *Indra* and *Brahmá*. *Dadhichi*, a worshipper of *Rudra*, was present, and declared that it was no sacrifice in which *Pashubhartti* or *Shiva* had not a share. *Daksha* replied: 'We have many *Rudras*, armed with tridents and wearing braided hair, who occupy eleven places, I know not *Maheshwara*.' While this dispute was going on, *Deví* instigated her husband to assert a claim to a share in the sacrifice, and *Mahádeva* accordingly created a dreadful being, who, attended by hosts of other frightful creatures, demolished all *Daksha's* preparations for the sacrifice. *Brahmá* and the other gods humbly enquired of this destroyer, who he was, to which he replied that he was neither *Rudra* nor *Deví*, but *Vírabhadra*, sent to destroy the sacrifice, and exhorted them to submit to *Mahadeva* 'whose wrath is better than the beneficence of any other god.' This is the legend to which Dr. Stevenson unhesitatingly refers the sculpture in this compartment; but it must be confessed the correspondence is slight, and consists only in the circumstance that it represents *Rudra* slaying a victim, which the Doctor would have to be *Daksha* held up by the "coronal tuft of hair." This theory must be discarded. Mr. Erskine and Dr. Wilson agree in calling the principal figure *Bhairava*—an *avatára* of *Rudra* and one of the most common objects of worship among the Maráṭhá people; and while the former suggests, the latter asserts that it represents a human sacrifice—that of a child.[90]

64. The whole attitude of the figure seems intended to express the more dark and horrid side of the character ascribed to *Shiva*, to which probably more prominence was given in early times when he was described as in the *Bhagavata Puráṇa*,—'roaming about in dreadful cemeteries, attended by hosts of ghosts 'and sprites, like a madman, naked, with dishevelled hair, laughing, weeping, 'smeared with the ashes of funeral piles, wearing a garland of dead men's '[skulls], and ornaments of human bones, pretending to be *Shiva* (auspicious) 'but in reality *Ashiva* (inauspicious), insane, beloved by the insane, the lord of '*Pramathas* and *Bhútas* (sprites) beings whose nature is essentially darkness.'[91] In this character he is called *Bhairava*—a name signifying 'horror;' *Kapálabhrit* or the 'skull-cherisher'—from his wearing a garland of them; *Mahákála* or Time personified as the great destroyer, &c. In the *Káliká Puráṇa* he is represented as giving instructions as to the celebration of human sacrifices, which, from a scene in *Bhavabhúti's* drama of *Málatí* and *Mádhava* already quoted, and from other

original sources, we know were sometimes perpetrated. And in this aspect he had a sect of followers known as *Kápálikas* or *Kápálas*, who went about as naked mendicants, smeared with funeral ashes, armed with a trident or a sword, with a string of human skulls hung round the neck, carrying one in the left hand, and half intoxicated with the spirits quaffed from this disgusting wine cup.[92] In the *Prabodha Chandrodaya* a *Kápálikà* is introduced with a sword in his hand thus soliloquising,—

"With goodly necklace deck'd of bones of men,
Haunting the tombs, with cups of human skull
Eating and quaffing,—ever I behold
With eyes that Meditations salve[93] hath clear'd,
The world of diverse jarring elements
Composed, but still all one with the Supreme.

* * * * * * *

"With flesh of men, with brain and fat well smear'd,
We make our grim burnt-offering,—break our fast
From cups of holy Bráhman's skull,—and ever
With gurgling drops of blood that plenteous stream
From hard throats quickly cut, by us is worshipped
With human offerings meet, our god, dread *Bhairava*.

* * * * * * * *

"With foaming floods of gore that gush amain
From throat well severed with thin sabre's edge,
I make my sacrifice to him that calls
With beat of drum the hosts of creatures after him
Dread *Shiva*—and with these rich ruddy streams
Delight his consort well, *Bhaváni*."[94]

Bhairava is still the special object of worship with the *Yogis* of Western India who represent these wild and fanatical devotees of former days, but they have laid aside the more revolting of their practices.

65. To the spectator's right, below, are some fragments of a male and two female forms; and above them, in a sort of recess, are two *ṛishis* with a very small figure in front, and above it a female. On the other side below there has been at least two dwarfs, and under *Rudra* a third figure. A small form also peers over the elephant's head.

66. Above the screen, in the centre, and immediately over the head of the principal figure, is a peculiar piece of carving not unlike the section of a very wide bottle with a curved groove in the middle of it. A similar form appears in some of the other sculptures, as twice in the fifth compartment, but not in so prominent a position: here, however, the figures on each side seem to be paying adoration to it, and antiquarians have puzzled themselves in vain to make out what it represents; Mr. Erskine is followed by Dr. Wilson in supposing it is the mystic triliteral syllable AUM—a sound not to be pronounced but meditated upon, as supposed to comprehend each individual of the Hindu triad, as if the essence of the religion were concentrated in it. But it is very difficult to

trace any resemblance between this figure and the syllable however peculiarly disguised, as it often is, in the writing.[95] Dr. Stevenson supposes it to represent the *linga*, but the resemblance is quite as unsatisfactory; nor can we quite agree with him that 'the rest of the gods seem petrified with horror,' nor yet with Dr. Wilson that the figures above are "represented with considerable art" and "in horror and amazement." At the foot of it, on each side, are two small fat prostrate figures; over the back of each are seen two figures apparently worshipping it—the pair nearest holding up clasped hands; the next, to the spectator's left, holds a garland; and that to the right holds up his hand before his forehead—both these, being the largest figures in the group, have their hair elaborately dressed, and wear necklaces, armlets, &c. Behind each of these last is a female figure floating jauntily with her feet turned up, and hanging on to the male in front of her.

67. Just in front of this compartment there may yet be traced a portion of the painted design or pattern that once graced the ceiling, and some of the plant and animal forms on it may still be made out,—among them the form of an elephant is distinct.

IX.—The Tándava Dance of Shiva.

68. The eighth compartment is that on the right side when entering the north portico (marked *G* on the plan). The principal figure again is *Shiva*, but here represented in a merrier mood, and apparently a favourite representation, as a copy of it also occurs at *Jogeshwari* in Salsette and also at *Elura*. The compartment is 10 feet 9 inches wide at the entrance and fully 13 feet inside, and 11 feet 2 inches high, raised on a low base. The figure of *Shiva* in the centre has been about 10 feet 8 inches in height, and has probably suffered a good deal during the past century, since from the account of Dr. W. Hunter, about 1783, it appears as if the first right and third left hand were then entire or nearly so: now only the fourth left hand remains. Like the other figures of *Shiva* it has had eight arms: the first right arm has passed across the body and been applied to the left side about the waist; the second was "thrown out from the body and the forearm has been bent," perhaps so as to bring the hand "before the breast, but is broken off a very little way beyond the elbow;" the forearm of the third is entirely gone, but it probably held the "sceptre" as De Couto calls it, but which Erskine styles "a *damdameh* or war-drum,"—though it more resembles the *parashu* or battle-axe; or perhaps it is a club or staff, round the top of which a cobra twists; the fourth arm is bent upwards, and touches this rod near the wrist, but the hand is broken off. The first two arms on the left side hang down, and are broken off near the wrists; the third is bent upwards but similarly injured; and the fourth is extended above the shoulder and

10. THE TANDAVA DANCE OF SIVA.

P. 38.

holds up a portion of his robe. The head-dress, secured by a band passing under the chin, is the usual high one, "so nicely made," says De Couto, "that it appears to have been painted rather than carved in stone with the chisel."[96] The right thigh is bent outwards, but broken off near the knee, and the left leg is entirely gone. With most of the surrounding figures it has been carved with more care than is displayed in many of the other sculptures. The armlets have been elaborately wrought, and are still sharp and distinct, as is also the belt or ribbon round the waist tied at the side, and its end fastened to a part of the robe which is spread over the right thigh. Under this girdle the edge of the robe, which has covered the lower portions of the figure, confines the stomach in a very natural way.

69. Dr. Stevenson will have it that this is *Bhairava*,[97] a form assumed by *Shiva* to put down the boasting of *Narasiṇha*, an *avatára* of *Vishṇu*, who claimed to be superior to *Shiva*, but he evades the want of evidence for this by supposing that "the artist thought it sufficient to exhibit the god in this form to assert his supremacy without irritating the numerous worshippers of *Vishṇu* as the supreme deity, by any humiliating mark of inferiority." This theory is more ingenious than probable;—it is only to make the sculptures agree with the *Liṅga Puráṇa* that it is called for, and the artist has nowhere else veiled the intention of his representations. It appears simply to have been intended to represent *Shiva* in a mood familiar to his votaries, and contrasting with that indicated in the last described and in the next sculpture, and for this their legends supplied abundant materials. These relate that, to amuse *Párvatí*, *Shiva* invented a particular kind of frantic dance, and taught it to *Taṇḍu*, one of his followers, whence it was called the *Táṇḍava*: this *Shiva* performed before the goddess and her sons, to the musical accompaniment of the tabor struck by his favourite *Nandi*. The peacock—the vehicle of *Kárttikeya* mistaking the deep sound of the drum for the rolling of thunder indicative of an approaching storm of rain, screamed with delight, and the snake which *Shiva* wears as a collar, alarmed at the notes of its mortal foe, deserted its place to make for a safe retreat. This is perhaps why we find it here on the top of *Shiva's parashu*. The legend says it made for *Gaṇapati's* trunk and all the bees that are supposed to settle on the temples of the elephant were thereby set a-buzzing. The author of the *Mudrá Rákshasa* speaks of the *Táṇḍava* as—"the dance of the "victor of *Tripura*—that dance to which space is wanting. Lightly treads the "god lest he should overset the earth—he cramps his action lest his arms reach "beyond the limits of the three worlds, and he bends his spark-emitting glances "on vacuity lest they should consume the objects on which they gaze."[98] This dance is said to be still practised by the *Shaiva* Brahmans in Karnáta.

70. To the left of *Shiva* is a female figure, 6 feet 9 inches high, probably *Párvatí*. She wears the same pendent from the necklace as in the marriage scene and other sculptures, large ear-rings, rich bracelets, and a girdle with carefully carved drapery, but her face and breasts are defaced. On her left has been another

female, but the breast and part of the arm only are left. Above *Párvati's* right shoulder is a flying female figure. Over this is *Vishṇu*, with his *gadá* or mace in one remaining hand, and the *shankha* or shell in the other, riding on the shoulders of *Garuḍa*, whose head is gone. In front of *Vishṇu*, and over the left hand of *Shiva*, is a male figure between two females, and behind these is a fourth figure—of which the face is gone—holding perhaps a water vessel. Over *Párvati's* left shoulder is *Indra* on his Elephant.

71. Below, at *Shiva's* right, is the skeleton form of *Bhringi*, much defaced; beside it is a fragment of a large object, probably a *mṛídanga* or tabor; and beyond this is a large male attendant with a high cap bearing a crescent and a skull, from the right eye of which a snake is crawling out: in his right hand he holds the *trishula* of *Shiva*, but it has lost two of its prongs. In front of him is a pretty large sitting figure, probably a musician. One of these two we may conclude to be *Nandi*. For *Bhringi's* presence we have again the authority of the *Kumára Sambhava*, where we read that—" *Bhringi* at the request of *Shiva* danced before her [*Umá*] " to please her, with wild and frightful gestures, with his large teeth and sharp " pointed hard beak. At the command too of her dear lord, *Kálí* danced with a " garland of the skulls of the dead about her neck and their faces looking hideous " with crooked teeth. Seeing these two dancing thus frantically before her, *Umá* " was terrified."[99]

72. Above the holder of the *trishula* is a pretty entire figure of *Gaṇesha* holding in his right hand a club and in his left his broken tusk. This figure still receives considerable attention by devotees, and is generally smeared over with red-lead, and often partially covered with gold leaf. To the left of the *trishula* bearer is the trunk of a female whose dress has been carefully and sharply cut even to its edges on her thigh. Higher up on a flat seat, carried by five *haṇsa* or geese, is *Brahmá* with three heads and four hands, in one of which he holds his water-vessel and the others are now broken off. De Couto says in his time the left hand of the central figure held a book,[100] and if we may trust to his accuracy in this, then the absence of the *Vedas* in the hands of *Brahmá* which has been remarked in the different figures of him, has probably arisen from mutilations, and when entire he was here represented, as in modern images, with the sacred texts in his hands. Between *Brahmá* and the head of *Shiva* are three figures, a male between two females,—the inner one holding some object like a dish; and behind *Brahmá* are two figures, one of which Erskine says is *Máruti*—a very questionable identification and not supported by the sculpture which does not well represent *Hanumán*: besides, he belongs rather to the *Vaishnava* mythology than to the *Shaiva*. Both these figures were probably intended for *Shaiva* devotees or sages. The one next to *Brahmá* wears his hair gathered up in a *jaṭá*.

II. SIVA AS MAHAYOGI.

P. 41.

X.—Shiva as Mahávogi, or Dharma Rája.

73. At the east end of this portico, and facing the last (at H on the plan), is a compartment that has greatly perplexed antiquarians, who have been unable to account for the resemblance borne by the principal figure to that of *Buddha* so frequent in the Cave Temples of his followers. But this may be due in part to the circumstance that the Brahmans excavated their cave temples in imitation and rivalry of the Bauddhas. The *bhikshus* or *Bauddha* ascetics wore yellow robes, and in imitation of them, probably, the *Shaiva yogis* and mendicants adopted tawny coloured clothes. *Buddha* was regarded by his followers as the Great Ascetic, and this may have tempted the early *Shaivas* to give prominence to a similar characteristic in the representation of their favourite object of worship.[101]

74. Not only in the character represented and the position given to the ascetic, does this figure resemble that of *Buddha*, but many of the minor accessories are scarcely disguised copies. The compartment has unfortunately been disgracefully defaced, and many of the details are now hopelessly obliterated. *Shiva* has had only two arms, both of them now broken off at the shoulder; he is seated cross-legged on a *padmásana* or lotus-seat, and the palms of his hands probably rested in his lap, between the upturned soles of the feet,[102] as in most images of *Buddha* and the *Jaina Tírthaṅkaras.* The stalk of the lotus forming the seat is upheld by two figures, shown only down to the middle, corresponding to the *nága*-canopied supporters of the *padmásana* of *Buddha.* The *mukuta* of *Shiva* has been carved with wonderful elaborateness; the front plate of the mitre-like crown is minutely engraved and has three knobs at the top, the central one round, and the side ones probably damaged forms; high up on the left side is the crescent; the ringlets that descend behind the head fall down on each shoulder; and at the back is the circular frill remarked on other statues, while around the whole is a large aureole like what we often find about the head of *Buddha.* The face, now much damaged, has had a very placid or perhaps contemplative aspect as befitting the character thus ascribed to him by the poet:—

> " Absorbed in holiest thought, erect and still,
> The Hermit rested on the gentle hill;
> His shoulders drooping down—each foot was bent
> Beneath the body of the Penitent;
> With open palms the hands were firmly pressed,
> As though a Lotus lay upon his breast;
> A double rosary in each ear—behind
> With wreathing serpents were his locks entwined;
> His coat of hide shone blacker to the view
> Against his neck of brightly beaming blue;
> How wild the look, how terrible the frown
> Of his dark eyebrows bending sternly down!

How fiercely glared his eyes, unmoving blaze
Fixed in devotion's meditating gaze!
Calm as a full cloud resting on a hill,
A waveless lake when every breeze is still,
Like a torch burning in a sheltered spot—
So still was he, unmoving, breathing not.

* * * *

At all the body's ninefold gates of sense
He had barred in the pure Intelligence,
To ponder on the Soul which sages call
Eternal Spirit, highest, over all."[103]

75. *Shiva* is said to have undertaken this penance when *Deví* or *Satí* his wife died, because she and her husband were not invited to her father *Daksha's* sacrifice. It is not to be expected therefore that she should figure here, though it is possible that, among his female attendants was—

"Fair *Umá* dwelling by the Hermit's side"—

For to him—

"The worship of a gift *Himálaya* paid,
And towards his dwelling sent the lovely maid;
Her task, attended by her youthful train,
To woo his widowed heart to love again."

The scene is laid in the *Himálaya* mountains, and the sculptor has caught some of the leading features of it as thus depicted by Kálidása :—

"High on that hill where musky breezes throw
Their balmy odours o'er the eternal snow
Where heavenly minstrels pour their notes divine
And rippling *Gangá* laves the mountain pine,
Clad in a coat of skin all rudely wrought
He lived for prayer and solitary thought;
The faithful band that served the Hermit's will
Lay in the hollows of the rocky hill,.
Where from the clefts the dark bitumen flowed;
Tinted with mineral dyes their bodies glowed,
Their garb, rude mantles of the birch-tree's rind,
With bright red garlands was their hair entwined."[104]

76. Above we have the heavenly minstrels, below the attendants are mostly seated as if among rocks, and to the left of *Shiva* is a plantain with three leaves expanded and the central germ rolled up, while under his left knee is the blossom of a sunflower. On each side stands a female *chámara*-bearer, and behind each a smaller female figure, but so defaced that we can determine little more than parts of their outlines. Below, on each side the plantain, sit two attendants, one of which has his ankles crossed; on the opposite side sits another with a rosary called *rudrákshamálá* of the berries of the *rudráksha*, employed by mendicant *Sanyásis* who are specially devoted to the worship of *Shiva*.[105] Over the plantain is *Vishṇu* riding on *Gáruḍa*, who has curly hair, and his wing streams up like ostrich feathers, but the faces of both are gone. Above *Vishṇu* is a figure on horse-

back; the head of the animal is gone, but the hoof, saddle, saddlecoth, girth, and bridle are distinct.[106] Behind this is a *ṛishi* with a rosary or *málá* in his hand. Between the horseman and *Shíva's* head are the usual celestial choristers floating in the clouds, the edges of the robes over the thighs of the two females being carefully carved, and the front one carries a *chámara;* while behind them is a fourth figure, of which the face is gone, holding what is perhaps meant for a water vessel. On the right side of the head are three similar figures—a male between two females—the former carrying what looks like a shell; and then comes a skeleton-like *ṛishi*, behind whom is *Brahmá* on his usual *váhana*, with his arms broken off. Below *Brahmá* is probably a representation of *Indra*, but his elephant has entirely disappeared. The other figures need not be particularized.

77. The only portions of this cave that have not been noticed above are the two cells at the ends of the recess in the back. They are a little above the level of the rest of the cave, and are entered by low doors. Both are very irregular: that on the east is 18 feet 1 inch by about 15 feet 9 inches,—the north and south sides differing by 6 inches; the other is 17 feet 6 inches from north to south, but the south side measures 14 feet 10 inches and the north 16 feet 3 inches. Both are very roughly hewn, and were probably used by the priests as storerooms.

XI.—The East Wing of the Great Temple.

78. By a neat flight of nine steps, 10 feet 10 inches wide, we descend from the eastern side of the Great Temple into a court fully 55 feet in width, which has been quite open to the north, but the entrance is now filled up to a considerable height by the earth and stones thrown out when this court was cleared some twenty years ago. The roof of the great cave projects about seven feet beyond the line of the pillars, and that of the smaller temple on the south side has similarly overhung the façade,—the rest has always been entirely open above. In the middle of the court is a circular platform,* only two or three inches in height and 16 feet 3 inches in diameter. It is directly in front of the shrine in the temple to the south, and also of that in the great cave to the west of it, and was most probably the position of the *Nandi* or great bull which always faces the *Linga* shrine; but no trace of it is known to exist now.

79. The Rock-temple on the south of this area is raised on a panelled basement about 3 feet 6 inches high, which again stands on a low platform 2 feet 4 inches in height. The front is about fifty feet in length and eighteen and a half feet

* Marked *l* on the plan.

in height from the platform. It was most probably divided into five spaces by four columns and two demi-columns; but of the former there are now only traces of the column in the west end of the façade—and of it only fragments of the base and capital remain, though twenty years ago the whole pillar was tolerably entire. The style of these pillars was the same as that in the Great Temple, their bases were 3 feet square, and they were surmounted by a plain architrave of two fascias, of which a small portion still remains. On the original basement are three courses of hewn stone, evidently of modern origin.

80. On each side the steps leading up to this temple are bases, and on that on the east or left side* is a tiger or leogriff, while beside the base on the right side, on a heap of earth, is its neighbour.† These figures sit upon their hind quarters, and each has the fore paw next to the steps raised. About three years ago the head of the former, which was more nearly finished than the other, was broken —probably by some seamen.

81. Inside, the *maṇḍapa* or portico of this temple measures 58 feet 4 inches by 24 feet 2 inches. At each end it has a chamber, and at the back the *garbha* or *Linga* shrine‡ with a *pradakshiṇá* or passage round it, varying from 8 feet 4 inches to 8 feet 9 inches in width. Five low steps and a threshold lead into the shrine, which is 13 feet 10 inches wide and 16 feet 1 inch deep. In the middle of the floor stands a low *vedi* or altar, 9 feet 5 inches square with the spout to the east. Into the middle of this is let a *Linga* 2 feet 5 inches in diameter and of the same compact stone as that in the *garbha* of the Great Temple. The door into this shrine is much damaged, but has been of a tasteful pattern: outside the two fascias of the jambs are two neat pilasters over the capitals of which runs a neat frieze, and round all a crenellated moulding.

82. At the back of the *maṇḍapa*, near the east end,§ is a gigantic statue or *dwárapála* with two attendant *pisháchas*. The whole is now much dilapidated: the principal figure has had four arms, and the *pishácha*, on his right, stands with his arms crossed, and has a snake knotted round the bottom of his abdomen, which rears its hood under his elbow. Near the west end‖ is a similar statue reaching nearly to the roof, with four arms, and the usual protuberance indicative of the third eye in the forehead; he has mustaches and a Roman nose now damaged; his hair is gathered up in a *jaṭá*, and in his left ear a snake is twisted and tied. He leans the elbow of his front left hand on a sort of ball placed on the head of the *pishácha;* the back hand is raised over his shoulder and holds up his robe; the front right hand is broken off, and the back one holds up a snake. Above, on each side of his head, is a fat flying figure like the cherubs so constantly found in *Bauddha* cave sculptures near the head of *Buddha*. Erskine thought this figure probably represented *Vírabhadra* or *Bhairava*.

83. At the west end of this portico is a small chapel 10 feet 10 inches in depth

* Marked *n* on the plan. † At *m* on the Plan. ‡ Marked *l* on the Plan.
§ At *o* on the Plan. ‖ At *p* on the Plan.

ELEPHANTA.

IV. Column in the Chapel E. of the Great Cave.

§ 83.

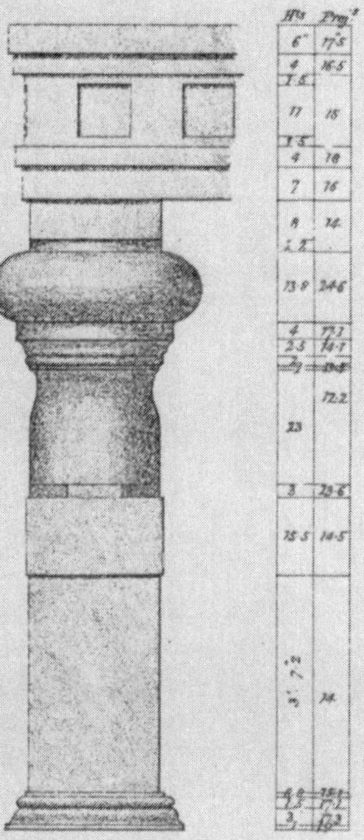

V. Kirtimukh.

§ 87.

1 Foot

Scale of 12 6 0 1 2 3 4 5 6 7 feet

J. Burgess, delt.

Government Litho: Press, Bombay 1871.

by about 25 feet in width inside. It has two pillars and two pilasters in front, and the floor being 1 foot 11 inches above that of the portico, it is entered by steps in front of the central opening. The pillars and pilasters are 10 feet 5½ inches in height. They are 2 feet 4 inches square, and of the same type as the pillars in the great cave, but have bases 7½ inches in depth, and no part of their capitals is fluted. Over them runs an entablature 2 feet 11 inches deep, consisting of five fascias of different breadths, the central one 1 foot 2 inches deep, having sunk panels about 11½ inches square and as much apart. Both the pillars are now broken through, and the northern one is almost entirely gone.* In the openings into this chapel there has been a railing with a door doubtless in the centre: the mortices for the ends of the bars are still visible in the bases and at the top of the square portions of the pillars, 5½ feet above the floor.

84. Inside, this chapel has been 'a chamber of imagery,' but it was probably often used in some late age as a cook room, and the smoke from the fires has covered the figures over with a sort of bark or scurf that hides any minuter features that may still be left: for they have been very roughly handled. At the south end† is a large figure of *Gaṇesha*. A squat figure on his right rests his head on the knee of the *deva*, whose hand lies on his neck. Another figure holds an offering, and has a cobra round his waist; above are two flying figures, and the usual three on each side as in other sculptures.

85. At the north end‡ is a standing figure holding in his hand the shaft of what was probably a *trishula;* his left hand rests on a defaced figure, perhaps a *pisháchа*. This is doubtless *Shiva* or *Shúlapáni*, 'the wielder of the trident.' On his right is *Brahmá* supported by his *haṅsas*, behind him is a monkey-faced dwarf, and above him three figures—the middle one a male holding an offering in his hands, as does also the female behind him. On the left of *Shúlapáni* is *Vishṇu* mounted on *Garuḍa*, and holding his mace in one of his right hands while the other is open. In one of his left hands he holds his *chakra*, and in the other his *Shankha* resting on the shoulder of *Garuḍa*. A male figure below holds the stalk of a lotus in his left hand, much as *Padmapáni* is represented in *Bauddha* sculptures; and between him and *Shiva* is a female with a *chámara*.

86. On the back wall of this chapel§ are sculptured ten principal figures,—the one at the north end being *Gaṇapatí*. Under them is a base 2 feet 7 inches high and of the same pattern as under the figures in the great cave. Most, if not all, of these figures seem to have represented females; several of them have had aureoles behind their heads; some of them carry children; and there are traces of at least five small figures below. Between each two of the first eight figures is a pole or staff surmounted by an ensign—a *haṅsa*, a peacock, a monkey, or other animal. It is difficult to say whom these may represent. Erskine and

* The drawing No. IV. will show the details and proportion of these pillars.

† At *K* on the Plan. ‡ At *L* on the Plan. § At *M* on the Plan.

Stevenson regard them as the *devânganá*—"the servants and dancing girls of the gods with *Ganésha* at their head."

87. Over this sculpture runs an architrave 2 feet 10 inches deep, and consisting of three plain members, the lower and upper projecting 5 inches from the line of the central band and rounded over above. The upper of these is divided into six equal spaces by five ornaments with two half ones at the ends, and the lower is divided by larger ornaments into five full spaces and two half spaces at the ends. These ornaments are all exactly similar to the well known Bauddha window-pattern ornament so common on the caves of *Ajanṭá*, *Kárla*, and elsewhere. Instead of being filled up with a human head or lattice work, however, they contain a fantastic face called a *Kírttimukha**—or 'Face of Fame.' The sunk frieze between the projecting members is 8 inches broad, and still retains the ground colours of the chequer pattern in which it has been painted.

88. Opposite this chapel, at the east end of the portico, is another, with two pillars and two pilasters in front, and similarly raised above the floor of the temple, but perfectly plain inside.† It measures 27 feet 7 inches by 11 feet 7 inches, and as the floor is sunk a few inches below the level of the plinth or step on which the pillars stand, the water that oozes into it through the rock above remains on the floor during most of the dry season. There is a tradition also that on the night of *Shivarátri*, the water of the Ganges comes through the roof, and the people of the island and from surrounding places flock to it on that occasion to enjoy the benefit of the miracle and to attend the fair then held.

XII.—The West Wing of the Great Temple.

89. Passing again through the Great Temple to its western side, we descend by a few steps into another court, the floor of which is filled up to some depth with fallen rock and debris. On this side also the roof of the great cave has projected some seven feet beyond the pillars of the portico, and the roof of the small chapel on the west side has projected five and a half feet: the rest of the court—about nineteen feet in width—has always been open above.[107] It had an entrance from the north, but it is now blocked up by earth and stones removed out of this court and the cave when it was cleared. On the south side is a cistern of considerable extent, the roof being supported by two rough-hewn square pillars of rock. It is now much filled up, and a large portion of the rock in front has fallen in; but originally it must have been on the plan of most Buddhist cisterns, of very considerable depth, with only a square opening above, near the east end: indeed De Couto relates that 'it was commonly said the bottom of it had never been found, and it is therefore like what is told of the fountains of

* See Drawing No. V. † At *N* on the Plan.

12. WEST WING OF THE GREAT CAVE.

D. H. Sykes Phot.

THE GREAT CAVE FROM THE EAST WING.

See Description §§. 78-88.

Alpheus and Arethusa.'[108] The water in it is very cool and palatable but somewhat alkaline.

90. The shrine on the west side of the court is entered through a portico* supported in front by two square pillars and two pilasters—now broken away, and approached by four or five steps before the central opening. This portico is about 27 feet in length, 13 feet 7 inches deep from the front of the platform, and 8 feet 10½ inches high. It contains a good deal of sculpture.

91. At the north end† is a group of figures very similar to that last described in the Great Temple.‡ In the centre is *Shiva*, in the ascetic attitude, on a lotus throne, the support of which is upheld by two fat figures with heavy wigs, and their bodies shown only down to the middle. Niebuhr's drawing represents *Shiva* as resting his left hand on his thigh and the right one slightly raised; the forearms are now broken off, but from the appearance of the bend at the elbow, we may believe this was their position. A similar figure at *Jogeshwari* holds a rosary in his right hand. To the right of *Shiva* is a figure sitting on his heels and holding an opening plantain; behind him is a bearded *muni* or sage, on the left is a similar sitting figure, and above is *Brahmá* with three faces, and some other forms; while in the clouds are four of the usual flying attendants on each side.

92. A door at the back of the portico leads into the *linga* shrine§ about 10 feet 7 inches by 9 feet 7 inches. In the centre is a *linga* 18 inches in diameter, placed in a *jhaládhara* or *vedi* nearly 6 feet square. On each side the door‖ is a *dwárapála* with two *pisháchas* at his feet and two fat flying figures above his shoulders.

93. To the south of this door¶ is a group of figures, among whom *Shiva* appears with six arms and the third eye in his forehead; his high *mukuta* is ornamented on the top of the right side with a crescent; in the front right hand he holds a Cobra; in the second, the *parashu* or club as in the dancing *Shiva;* and the third or outer arm is broken off. In his front left hand he holds a portion of his dress; in the second is some object now defaced; and the palm of the third is exposed. At his right is a plantain tree with a figure sitting on the ground, and above is *Brahmá* on his lotus-seat borne by the *hañsas*. On *Brahmá's* left is a male riding on a bull with a bell attached to its neck, and between this and *Shiva's* head are two figures, one of them a female holding a *chámara*. Beside *Shivá's* front left arm is a female figure with a drop on her forehead and neatly looped head-dress; above her left shoulder is *Indra* on *Airavati*, and behind him *Vishṇu* with four arms holding his *chakra* in one of his left hands and riding on the shoulders of *Garuḍa*, who is marked with the *tilaka* on his forehead. In front of *Garuḍa's* wing is a small flying figure, and beneath is a male with a crescent in his hair.

94. At the south end of this portico is a small rude chamber**—or rather

* Marked *O* on the Plan. † At *P* on the Plan. ‡ See § 73-76. § At *Q*
‖ At *q* and *r* on the Plan. ¶ At *R* on the Plan. ** Marked *S* on the Plan.

the beginning of one—for it is quite rough and scarcely large enough to contain more than one person.

95. Such, after the vicissitudes of a thousand years, is the Great Rock-Temple of Elephanta; the hand of Time has, on the whole, dealt gently by it; and the iconoclasm of *Islám*, so far as we know, lifted no hand against it; to the *Feringi* from the far west it was left to begin and to continue its wanton destruction. What it was like in the days of its glory we are left to imagine. De Couto, writing in 1603, says:—" The rock of the hill in which the Temple is carved is of " a dark-grey colour, but the entire body inside, the columns, the statues, and " everything else was formerly covered with a thin coating of lime mixed with a " sort of bitumen and other preparations, which made the temple altogether so " bright that it was a beautiful object and well worth seeing; and not only did " it make the figures very pretty, but enabled one to perceive very distinctly the " features of the countenances and the delicacy of the workmanship: so that " neither in silver nor in wax could they be made or engraven with more nicety " nor with more elegance and perfection." But again, " this temple," he says, " is injured in many parts, and what has been spared by the soldiers is so badly cared " for that it is a great pity to see thus destroyed one of the most remarkable things " in the world. It is now fifty years since I went to see this strange Temple; " and as I did not enter it with that curiosity with which I might do so now, " I did not remark many things that do not now exist."[109] Fragmentary traces of the painting on the roof are still discernible in the west and north porches, and other indications may be found in the last described wing and elsewhere in support of De Couto's account of the whole having been coated with a light coloured pigment. The mutilations must speak for themselves.

THE SECOND ROCK TEMPLE.

96. A short distance to the south-east of the Great Temple and at about the same level, is the second excavation,* facing E.N.E. Its extreme length is about a hundred and nine and a half feet, inclusive of the chapel at the north end. The façade, however, is so completely destroyed, the entrance so filled up with a bank of earth and debris, and the interior so injured by the water thereby retained inside, that it is difficult to form a proper estimate of the appearance it presented when entire. The front was nearly 80 feet in length, and must have been supported by a number of columns with two demi-columns at the ends, of which latter some fragments still remain. Inside, the portico or *maṇḍapa* extended five feet further to the south, giving a total length of 85 feet, with a depth of about 35 feet. At the north end of this is a chapel raised a few feet above the level of the *maṇḍapa*, supported in front by four octa-

* See Drawing No. VI.

ELEPHANTA.

VI. PLAN of CAVE II. See §§ 96, 97.

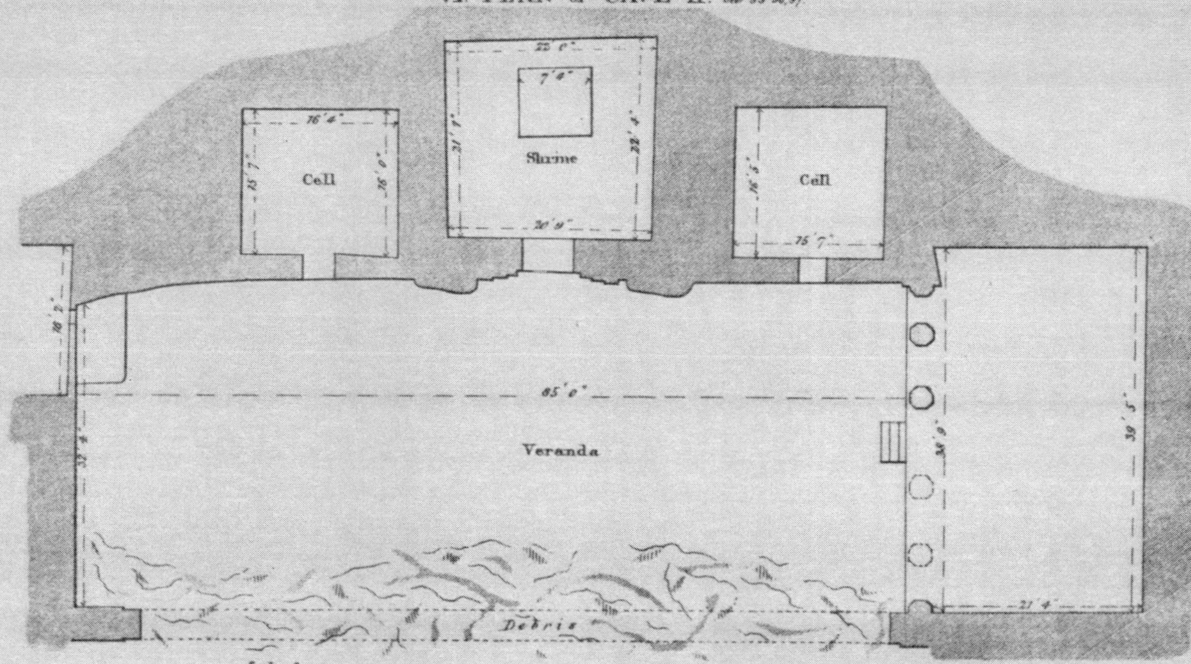

J. Burgess, delt.

Government Litho Press, Bombay 1871.

ELEPHANTA.

VII. PLAN of CAVE III.

See §§ 98-100

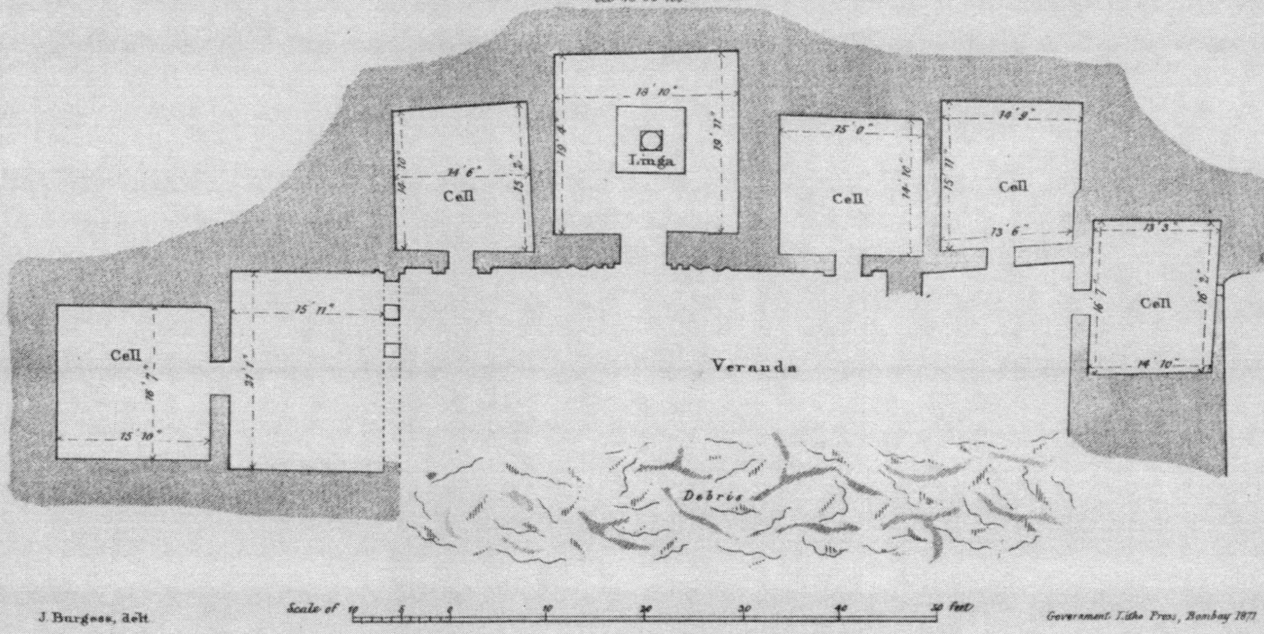

J. Burgess, delt.

Government Litho Press, Bombay 1877

gonal columns and two demi-columns about 2 feet 9 inches in diameter, slightly tapering upwards, and with capitals much resembling those in the great cave, except that the compressed-cushion member was not proportionately so deep nor projected so far, and it was crowned by a fluted cyma-recta terminated by a fillet over which lay a very thin abacus. Of these pillars two are entirely gone. The chapel inside is about thirty-nine feet in width by twenty-two in breadth, but, like most other apartments, its opposite sides do not measure exactly alike. It is perfectly plain inside. At the back of the portico are three chambers: that to the north is about 15 feet 9 inches wide by 16 feet 5 inches deep, and is generally, even throughout the dry season, filled with water to a depth of several inches. The corresponding one near the south end is similar.

97. The central chamber is 20 feet 9 inches wide in front and 22 feet at the back, by 21 feet 1 inch deep on the left and 22 feet 4 inches on the right; and about three feet from the back wall stands a *vedi*, 7 feet 4 inches square, with the *pranálíká* to the north,—the *linga* however has disappeared. At the entrance to this shrine is the only sculpture in the cave. The door is 5 feet 4 inches wide, and the architrave and jambs measure about 5 feet 10 inches: the inner members resemble those round the door of the shrine in the east wing of the Great Temple and in the fourth cave; outside these is a leaf moulding all round, and then a thick torus. Over the door the sculpture has mostly fallen down; but at the head of the jambs two figures of animals perform the part of brackets.[110] On the frieze above are some figures—those in the centre not easily made out, then a long *makara* with a fantastic sort of tail, then a boy holding back the upper lip of a second *makara*, and at each end a fat figure. Outside the jambs on each side stood a lofty *dwárapála*, over whose shoulders are two flying figures—a male and a female. But from the water having no escape from this cave, it has of late gone rapidly to ruin and the *dwárapálas* are mere fragments.

THE THIRD ROCK-TEMPLE.

98. At the south end of the portico of the second cave is a large block of rock not hewn away, above which is a hole through a thin partition of rock into one of the cells of the third Rock-Temple. The entrance to it, however, is a little further to the south. This cave is still more dilapidated than the last. The width of its *maṇḍapa* or portico can scarcely be determined;* the length inside was about 50 feet 2 inches. At each end there seems to have been a chapel or room with pillars in front: that at the north end 15 feet 7 inches deep, with a cell at the back, whose mean dimensions are 14 feet deep by 16 feet 4 inches

* See Drawing VII.

wide, and a second on the west side measuring 13 feet 6 inches in front and 14 feet 9 inches at the back, with a mean depth of 15½ feet. The chapel at the south end is 21 feet 1 inch by 15 feet 11 inches, and has a cell at the back measuring 15 feet 10 inches by 16 feet 7 inches, but almost filled up with earth. A pilaster and portion of a pillar in front of this chapel show that they were octagonal and of the same style as those in the second cave.

99. Like the last, this cave has also suffered from the water that accumulates in it during the rains, and which has no way of escape. The door in the centre of the back of the portico leading into the shrine has suffered much from this cause: it is 4 feet 9 inches wide and of similar pattern to the others with large *dwára-pálas* at each side, leaning on dwarfs, and with two flying figures over the head of each. The jamb and architrave measure 2 feet 3 inches in breadth and the *dwárapálas* and *pisháchа* on each side occupy 5 feet more.

100. The shrine inside is a plain room 19 feet 10 inches deep by 18 feet 10 inches wide with a low *vedi* or altar 6 feet 11 inches square, containing a *Liṅga*, 6 feet 11 inches in circumference or 23 inches in diameter. On each side is a cell, about 15 feet square, entering from the portico by doors which have projecting pilasters and ornamental pediments. They are much destroyed, but the horse-shoe ornament, so frequent in the Buddhist caves, is repeated several times and forms the principal feature.

THE FOURTH ROCK-TEMPLE.

101. Crossing the ravine in front of the first three caves and ascending the opposite hill to a height of upwards of a hundred feet above the level of the Great Temple, we come to a fourth excavation,* bearing nearly E. N. E. from it, spoken of by Dr. Wilson in 1850, as "discovered by Mr. Trotter a few years ago;" but it is thus described by De Couto:—"In the other hill of this small island, "to the east, beyond the Great Temple, and nearly in the centre, is another temple "to which the entrance was formerly by a beautiful gate, which had a porch of "marble most exquisitely wrought. This temple has a large hall and three "chambers: in the first, to the right hand, there is nothing left now; the second "has two idols seated on a large square seat. One of these idols was called "*Vithalá Chendai*, had six arms, and only one head, and was supported by two "small idols that were on each side of it." Possibly he meant *Vetála* and *Chandí* —but the images have long since disappeared.[110] This temple is now known to the natives of the island as *Sitabai's Déwala*.

102. The portico has four pillars and two pilasters 8 feet 5 inches high,

---

* See Plan No. VIII.

ELEPHANTA.

VIII. PLAN of CAVE IV.

See §§ 101–104.

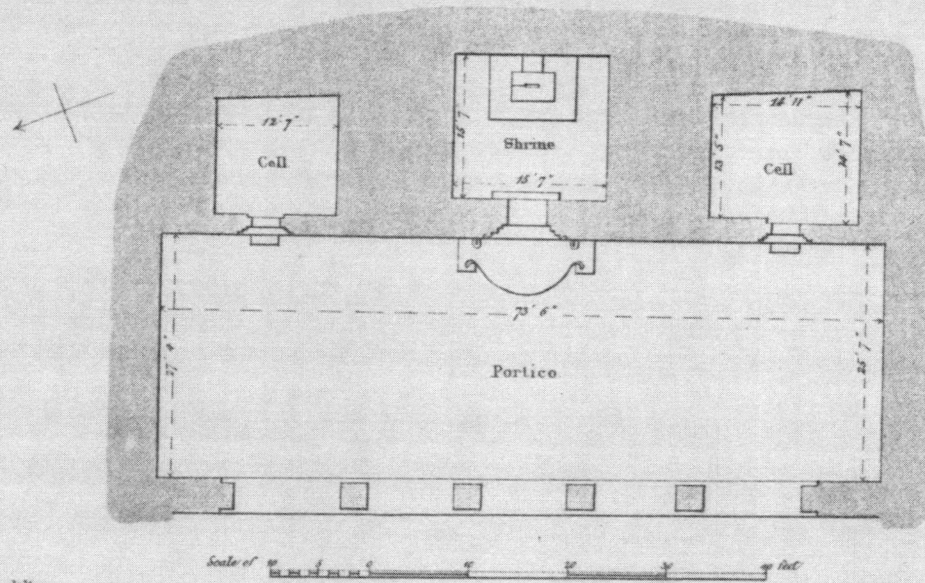

J Burgess, delt.

Government Litho Press, Bombay 1877

ELEPHANTA.

X. Door of the Cells in Cave IV. § 103.

IX. Column in the Veranda.
Cave IV. § 102.

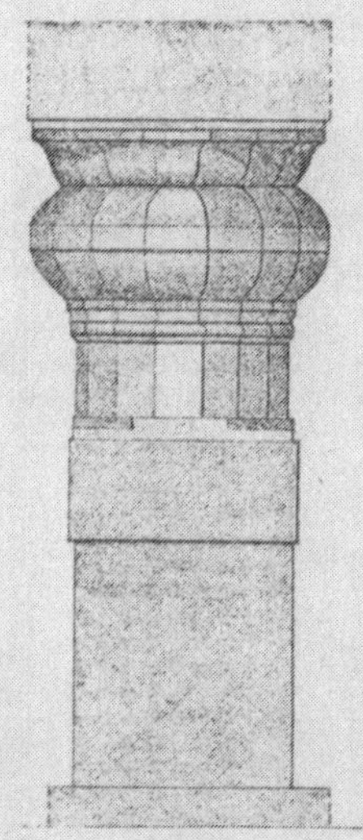

Scale of 12 6 0 1 2 3 4 5 6 7 Feet

J. Burgess, delt. — Government Litho Press, Bombay 1871.

and about 3 feet square at the base. The style of moulding is similar to those of the columns in the other caves, but the proportions differ somewhat; they are square to a height of 4 feet 6½ inches from the step on which they stand; a fillet of 1½ inches is octagonal, and above this they are sixteen sided with the exception of a thin crowning member of 1½ inches, which is square.*

103. Owing doubtless to this temple being so little known, though it is resorted to by cattle for shelter, it has scarcely suffered from violence. It faces W. N. W., and the ground is level for some distance in front. Where the declivity begins there are traces of a wall and some squared stones,—possibly indicative of the locality of the entrance gate of which De Couto speaks. The *maṇḍapa* is 73 feet 6 inches long, and 27 feet 4 inches wide at the north end, and 25 feet 7 inches at the south. The two side cells are perfectly empty. They have very neat doors;† one jamb of the northern one, however, has fallen away, owing to a flaw in the rock. The entrance is 2 feet 11 inches wide by 6 feet 5 inches high, and is approached by two steps of 8 inches high and a threshold of 4 inches. Round the jambs is an architrave 4⅝ inches wide with a simple moulding, and then a band, 6¾ inches broad, with a neatly wrought crenellated ornament reaching to within 1 foot 6½ inches of the step. The northern cell is roughly 12 feet 7 inches square; the southern 14½ by 15 feet.

104. The central chamber is the shrine and the door into it has neat pilasters and a frieze.‡ The entrance is 7 feet 11 inches high and 3 feet 11¼ inches wide. Besides the threshold of 4 inches and a step of 7½ inches, it has in front a semi-circular low step 2 inches in height, at the ends of which have been the heads of two lions;—these are the only portions that seem to have been wilfully damaged. This shrine has a mean depth of 15½ feet by 15¾ feet wide; and 20 inches from the wall, to which it is partially attached by a portion of the rock not hewn away, is a *vedi* or altar 4 feet 5 inches by 3 feet 5 inches and 3 feet 4 inches in height, neatly moulded, and standing on a low platform a few inches in height and 7 feet 2½ inches by 8 feet 10½ inches. It has a *prandlikâ* to the north. There is a hollow in the top a few inches deep and 17 inches long by 6 inches wide;—whether the images spoken of by De Couto were fixed in it or not is not easy to determine.

105. About a hundred and fifty yards to the north of this last, is a small excavation, being little more than the commencement of what was perhaps intended for three cells, but, as remarked by Dr. Stevenson, "the work seems to have been stopped before any material progress had been made."

106. Still farther on, to the north-east and just under the summit, are three wells cut in the rock, with openings about 2½ feet square, similar to the cisterns found beside many Bauddha excavations. Near these are some brick foundations,

---

* See the drawing IX. † See the drawing No. X. ‡ See the drawing No. XI.

and on the summit of this hill are the remains of an old fortification. Underneath this, and not far from the shore, is a fine large well, cut in the solid rock, and most easily reached by going along the strand. Near it was lately to be seen the torso of a statue of hard bluish stone, apparently only recently broken.

107. To the south of the second and third cave, at some distance, is a large cavern dark and infested with bats, that has been very roughly excavated,—more in the style of a cistern indeed than a Temple. The entrance is almost choked up with earth.

108. At the south end of the ravine that runs across the island is a tank, by the side of which is at least one *liṅga*, and it is said that a few years ago they were numerous.

109. Again, on the summit, to the west of the Great Temple, there is a figure of a tiger broken, however, into several pieces—which the natives seem to revere as *Umá Wágeshwarí*, or *Devi* in the form of a tiger. It much resembles those at the steps to the east wing of the Great Temple, and is probably one of those that once stood at the main entrance. It stands about 3 feet high and is 1 foot 9 inches across the hams, with a collar round the neck; but it is split into several pieces that are however placed together so as to preserve the figure. Dr. Wilson remarks that it is mentioned in the twenty-ninth chapter of the first section of the *Sahyádrí Khanḍ* of the *Skanḍa Puráṇa.**

---

* *Jour. Bomb. B. R. As. Soc.* Vol. III. pt. ii. p. 42.

ELEPHANTA.

XI. DOOR of the SHRINE in the IVth CAVE.

§ 104.

J. Burgess, delt.

Government Litho. Press, Bombay 1871.

NOTES.

1) §. 1. The principal notices of Elephanta are in the following works :—1. J. H. Van Linschoten (1579), *Discourse of Voyages*, (London, 1598) Boke I. ch. 44. p. 80. 2. Diogo de Couto, (1603) *Da Asia*, Decada VIIma. liv. iii. cap. 11. (Ed. Lisboa, 1778) tom. VII. pp. 250-261 ; also translated in *Jour. Bomb. Br. R. As. Soc.* vol. I. pp. 41-45. 3. Fryer, (1673) *New Account of East India and Persia*, p. 75. 4. J. Ovington, *Voyage to Suratt in the year* 1689, pp. 158-161. 5. Capt. A. Hamilton, *New Account of the East Indies*, (ed. 1744). vol. I. pp. 241-242. 6. Capt. Pyke, (1712), " Account of a Curious Pagoda near Bombay," extracted from his Journal by A. Dalrymple, Esq., F. R. & A.S., *Archæologia*, vol. VII. pp. 323-332. 7. J. H. Grose, *Voyage to the East Indies begun in* 1750, (2 vols. 8vo. Lond. 1766) vol. I. pp. 59-62. 8. Ives, *Voyage from England to India in* 1754, p. 45. 9. Anquetil du Perron, *Zend-Avesta*, Discours preliminaire, tom. I. pp. ccccxix-ccccxxiii. 10. C. Niebuhr, (1764) *Voyage in Arabie et en d'autres pays circonvoisons*, tom. II. pp. 25-33 ;—this account is illustrated by nine plates, but the relative sizes and positions of the figures are often incorrect. 11. Dr. W. Hunter—in *Archæologia* vol. VII. pp. 286-295. 12. Hector Macneil, (1783),—*Archæologia*, vol. VIII. pp. 270-77. 13. Goldingham (1795), *Asiatic Researches*, vol. IV. pp. 409-17. 14. Forbes, *Oriental Memoirs*, vol. I. pp. 423, 432-35, 441-48. 15. Mrs. Graham, *Journal of a Residence in India*, pp. 45-51. 16. Lord Valentia, *Travels*, (4to. ed.) vol. II. pp. 199-200. 17. Moor, *Hindu Pantheon*, pp. 49, 59, 97-98, 241-49, 334-36. 18. Sir W. Ouseley, *Travels in the East*, vol. I. pp. 81-95. 19. W. Erskine, *Transactions of the Literary Society of Bombay*, vol. 1. pp. 198-250 ;—a very minute description with good illustrations by Mrs. Ashburner, Capt. Basil Hall, and others. This account was reprinted with four very rude wood-cuts in *The Bombay Agenda or Almanac and Directory* for 1845, pt. ii. pp. 135-58. 20. Capt. Basil Hall, *Asiatic Journal*, 1816, vol. II. pp. 546-48. 21. Lieut.-Col. Fitzclarence, *Journal of a Route across India*, &c., pp. 321-22. 22. Heber, *Journal*, (4to. ed.) vol. II. pp. 179-83. 23. Fergusson, *Rock-Cut Temples of India*, pp. 54-55 ; and *Jour. R. Asiat. Soc.* vol. VIII. pp. 83-84. 24. Dr. J. Wilson, *Jour. Bomb. Br. R. Asiat. Soc.* vol. III. pt. ii. pp. 41, 42 ; vol. IV. pp. 341-342 ; and *Calcutta Review*, vol. XLII. (1866) pp. 1-25. 25. Dr. Stevenson, *Jour. Bomb. Br. R. As. Soc.* vol. IV. pp. 261-275 ; this is a résumé of Erskine's description with illustrative notes from the *Linga Purana*. 26. Lady Falkland, *Chow-Chow*, vol. I. pp. 109-114. 27. Gough, *Comparative View of the Ancient Monuments, of India, particularly those in the Island of Salset near Bombay* (4to, London 1785) :—this consists of reprints of the accounts of Linschoten, Fryer, Ovington, Capt. Hamilton, Pyke, Grose, du Perron, and Niebuhr. In Grindlay's *Scenery, &c. of Western India*, there are four plates of the Great Cave, drawn by Westall in 1803, with descriptive extracts from Erskine's account ; in Daniell's *Views* there are also some plates of the same ; and in various Encyclopædias, Histories, &c. there are accounts founded on those above enumerated.

2) §. 2. Ghárápuri घारापुरी, is sometimes also vulgarly called Gáripuri. Du Perron writes the name Galipouri, which is followed by Niebuhr. Dr. Stevenson will have it to be Gárápuri, which he translates as "Town of Excavations," and Dr. J. Wilson suggests that Ghárápuri may possibly mean " Hill of Purification."

3) §. 2. Captain Pyke, of the 'Stringer' E. Indiaman, afterwards Governor of St. Helena, who visited the Island in 1712, mentions that the Elephant had a smaller one on its back, and a sketch of it is given in one of the plates accompanying his account. (*Archæologia* Vol. VII.) as also of the stone horse a little further up the valley, and which is mentioned by Fryer in 1673, and by Ovington in 1689. Anquetil du Perron speaks of the smaller elephant as existing in 1760, whereas Grose, who preceded him, says "on the back of the Elephant was placed standing another young one appearing to have been all of the same stone, but it has been long broken down," and the accurate Niebuhr says "it bears some object on its back, but time has rendered it quite unrecognisable.' In 1813, Mr. Erskine writes—"the remains of its four paws, as well as the marks of the junction of its belly with the back of the larger animal, were perfectly distinct;" and Captain Basil Hall adds that "the smaller figure on the top of the elephant cannot have been a young elephant; it must have represented some animal capable of being placed in a sprawling attitude: it gives the idea of a tiger with its limbs extended so as to embrace the elephant's back and the whole belly of the tiger brought into contact with the elephant. It is inconceivable how an elephant (as it is said to have been) could possibly bring itself to this posture. The two hind feet present an appearance of hoofs; the right fore-foot is entirely gone; the left fore-foot is more extended—advancing too further towards the great elephant's head than the right."

Mr. Erskine gives the following dimensions of the large elephant :—

	ft.	in.
Length from the forehead to the root of the tail	13	2
Height at the head	7	4
Circumference of the whole animal at the height of the shoulders	35	5
" " animal round the four legs	32	0
Breadth of the back across the rump	8	0
Girth of the body about the middle	20	2
Height of the left hind foot	5	6
Circumference of the right fore foot	6	7½
" " right hind foot	6	8
" " left hind foot	7	7
" " left fore foot	7	3
Height of the supporter left in the stone to sustain the belly	2	2
Length of the tail	7	9
Circumference of the tail	2	10
Distance from the top of the brow to the curve of the trunk	5	3
Length of the trunk from between the tusks	7	10
Right tusk	0	11
Left tusk	0	6

The dimensions of the remains of the figure on the back of the elephant were :—

	ft.	in.
Length of the smaller animal	4	7
Distance of the two hind hoofs	3	6
Breadth of the body	1	2

4) §. 3. "A Voyage to Suratt in the year 1689, by J. Ovington, M.A., Chaplain to His Majesty"—p. 158.

5) §. 3. Hamilton's *New Account of the East Indies*, Vol. I. p. 241.

6) §. 4. The ascent to the cave was constructed by Karamsi Ranmal, a Lohana merchant of Bombay, in 1853-54 at an expense of about Rs. 12,000. The stone used was all carried over from Bombay. He built also the temple at the Baikala Railway Station,

in Bombay, a Dharmashala at Ghoḍabandar, a tank at Panwel, and a paved ascent at Trimbak.

7) §. 5. Fergusson's *Rock Cut Temples*, pp. 52 and 54. The Dumar Léná is the largest of the Elura Caves, and measures 150 feet each way. It is supported by twenty-six pillars, with pilasters at the angles, almost exactly like those of Elephanta. "The sculptures, too," says Mr. Fergusson, "seem intended to have been nearly the same, and on one side the entrance we find the same figure of Buddha, or, as the people call him here, Jam Dharma, the Dharma Raja, which puzzles the antiquarian at Elephanta." conf. Sykes' *Trans. Bomb. Lit. Soc.* vol. III. p. 272.

8) §. 10. Fergusson, *History of Architecture*, vol. II. pp. 499-501.

9) §. 12. De Couto mentions that in his time many of the sculptures had been broken "by the frolic of the soldiers of the fleet that visited the place," and adds—"what was spared by the soldiers, is so badly cared for, that is grievous to see thus destroyed one of the most wonderful things in the world;" and from the way in which he speaks of its having been defaced in his own time, we may well infer that it had then only recently ceased to be used. (See §. 95.) Linschoten visited it in 1579, and writes—"these *Pagodes* and build- "ings are now whollie left overgrowne, and spoyled, since the Portingales had it under their subjection." Fryer, in 1673, says it was "defaced by the Portugals who have this island also;" and Pyke in 1712 says—"The Portuguese now fodder all their cattle there in the rainy seasons "and to defend them from the violence of the monsoons: and lately one of their Fidalgos, "to divert himself with the echo which is here most admirable, fired a great gun into it "with several shot, which has broken some of the pillars." Grose evidently found this latter circumstance remembered, but materially exaggerated in his time: he says the figures "had "also continued in a tolerable state of preservation and wholeness, considering the remoteness "of their antiquity, until the arrival of the Portuguese, who made themselves masters of the "place, and in the blind fury of their bigotry, not suffering any idols but their own, they "must have been at even some pains to maim and deface them, as they now remain, consi- "dering the hardness of the stone. It is said they even brought field pieces to the demolition "of the images, which so greatly deserved to be spared for the unequalled curiosity of "them." Du Perron had perhaps jumbled his information when he wrote—'When the 'Maráthas had recovered Salsette, in order to cause the plaster with which the Portuguese had 'covered many of the figures to fall off, they dragged some pieces of cannon into the tem- 'ples of *Montpesir* and *Elephanta* which caused parts of the bas-reliefs to fall off with the 'plaster. Observing this effect they ceased firing, and took to clearing the figures by free- 'ing them of the plaster with a mallet.'—*Zendav.* tom. I. p. cccxxii.

10) §. 13. The Shivarátri is regarded by the *Shaivas* as 'the most sacred of all their observances, expiating all sins, and securing the attainment of all desires during life, and union with Shiva or final emancipation after death.' The ceremony is said to have been enjoined by Shiva himself, who declared to his wife Umá that the 14th of Phálguna vad (dark half of the month), if observed in honour of him, should be destructive of the consequences of all sin, and should confer final liberation. According to the *'Ishána Sanhitá*, it was on this day that Shiva first manifested himself as a marvellous and interminable Linga to confound the pretensions of both Brahmá and Vishṇu who were disputing which was the greater divinity. To decide the quarrel, they agreed that he should be acknowledged the greater, who should first ascertain the limits of the extraordinary object which appeared of a sudden before them. Setting off in opposite directions, Vishṇu undertook to reach the base, Brahmá the summit; but after some thousand years of the

gods, both returned from the fruitless attempt, 'and confessed the vast superiority of Shiva.' The legend seems to typify the exaltation of the *Shaiva* worship over that of Vishṇu and Brahmá, an event which no doubt at one time took place. 'According to some, the ceremony should begin on the evening of the 13th *tithi*, or lunar day, if it extends to four hours after sunset; according to others it should begin on the 13th or 14th *tithi*, according as one or other comprises the larger proportion of the hours of the night. Others hold that the *tithi* which comprises both evening twilight and midnight is the proper one, and others again that which includes midnight without the evening.' These are knotty points: they are such however as ritualists concern themselves most about.

'The three essential observances are fasting during the whole *tithi*, or lunar-day, and holding a vigil (*jagaraṇa*) and worshipping the Linga during the night; but the ritual is loaded with a vast number of directions for the presentation of offerings to the Linga, for gesticulations to be employed, and prayers to be recited to various inferior divinities connected with Shiva, and to Shiva in his various forms. After bathing in the morning, the worshipper recites his *Sankalpa*, or pledges himself to celebrate the worship. He repeats the ablution in the evening, and going afterwards to a temple renews his pledge, saying "I will perform "the worship of Shiva in the hope of accomplishing all my wishes, of obtaining long life "and progeny, and wealth, and for the expiation of all sins of whatever dye I may have "committed during the past year, open or secret, knowingly or unknowingly, in thought, "or act or speech." He then scatters mustard-seed with special *mantras* and offers an argha (or oblation of eight ingredients); after which he goes through the mátṛika nyása,—to a set of gesticulations accompanied by short mystical prayers, consisting chiefly of un-meaning syllables, preceded by a letter of the alphabet: as, "A-kam, 'A-srán, salutation to the thumb; I-chan, 'I-sṛin, salutation to the forefinger; U-stan, 'U-stúm, salutation to the middle finger;" and so on, going through the whole alphabet with a salutation or *namaskar'* to as many parts of the body, touching each in succession, and adding as the *mantras* proceed, names of the Mátṛis, female Shaktis or energies of Shiva, who by virtue of these incantations, are supposed to take up their abode for the time in the different members of the worshipper. Other objects are supposed to be effected by similar means; impediments are obviated by stamping thrice and repeating as often the *mantra*—"Haun, to the weapon, phaṭ;" next, with the same *mantra*, and by thrice snapping the finger, the ten quarters of the sphere or universal space, are aggregated in the Linga; and the purification of all beings is to be effected by thrice clapping the hands together, and uttering the same *mantra* each time. The repetition of nyása or touching parts of the body, whilst repeating mystical ejaculations, accompanies every offering made to the Linga, during the whole ceremony. In the first watch of the night on which the vigil is held, the linga is to be bathed with milk, the worshipper, or Brahman employed by him, uttering the *mantra* "Haun, reverence to 'Ishána." An offering is then made with the prayer:—"Devoutly "engaging in thy worship, O 'Ishwara, and in repeating thy names, I celebrate the "Shivarátri rite according to rule, do thou accept this offering!" Incense, fruits, flowers, boiled rice, &c., or sometimes even dressed flesh are offered with the customary prostration, and with the repetition of other *mantras*. A similar course is followed in the other three periods with a modification of the formulæ, and the articles used to bathe the Linga with. Thus in the second, it is bathed with curds, with the *mantra* "Haun-—reverence to Aghora;" and the *mantra* of the *argha* is,—"Reverence to the holy Shiva, "the destroyer of all sins; I offer this *argha* at the Shivarátri, do thou with "Umá be propitious." In the third, the bathing is with *ghi*, with the *mantra* "Haun, "reverence to Vámadeva;" and the *argha-mantra* is,—"I am consumed with pain, poverty, "and sorrow: oh, lord of Parvati, do thou, O beloved of Umá, accept the argha

"I present thee on this Shivarátri!" In the fourth watch the Linga is bathed with honey, with the *mantra* "Haun, reverence to Sadyojata;" and the *argha-mantra* is,—"Oh Shankara! take away the many sins committed by me, accept beloved of Umá, "the oblation I present thee on this night of Shiva." At daylight, the ceremony is concluded with the radical *mantra*, "Shiváya namaḥ" and some such prayers as these: "Through thy favour, O Ishwara! this rite is completed without impediment; O look "with favour, O lord of the universe, Hara, sovereign of the three worlds, on what I have "done this day which is holy and dedicated to Rudra! Through thy grace has this rite "been accomplished. Be propitious to me, O thou most glorious! Grant to me increase "of affluence: merely by beholding thee I am assuredly sanctified." Oblations to fire are then made, and the ceremony concludes with further offerings to the Linga and with the *mantra*, "By this rite may Shankara be propitiated, and coming hither, bestow the eye "of knowledge on him who is burnt up by the anguish of worldly existence." The yajamána or worshipper is then required to feast the Brahmans and make presents to them.—Abridged from H. H. Wilson, *Jour. R. Asiat. Soc.* vol. IX. pp. 91-95; *Works*, vol. II. pp. 211-216.

11) §. 15. The light in which at one time the Vaishnavas regarded the followers of Shiva is well illustrated in the following extract from the first Adhyaya of the *Vasishtha-smriti*:—"A Brahman versed in the four Vedas, who does not find Vásudeva [*Krishna* an avatara of Vishṇu,] is a donkey of a Brahman, trembling for the heavy burden of the Veda. Therefore, unless a man be a Vaishṇava, his Brahmahood will be lost; by being a Vaishṇava one obtains perfection, there is no doubt. For Náráyaṇa (Vishṇu) the highest Brahman, is the deity of the Brahmans; Soma, Súrya, and the rest, are the gods of Kshatriyas and Vaishyas; while Rudra and similar gods ought to be sedulously worshipped by the Shúdras. When the worship of Rudra is enjoined in the *Puranas* and law-books, it has no reference to Brahmans, as Prajápati declared. The worship of Rudra and the Tripuṇḍra (the three horizontal marks across the forehead) are celebrated in the *Puranas*, but only for the castes of the Kshatriyas, Vaishyas, and Shúdras, and not for the others. Therefore, ye excellent Munis, the Tripuṇḍra must not be worn by Brahmans." Conf. Max Müller, *Hist. Sansk. Liter.* pp. 55, 56.

12) §. 15. Shambhu is from *Sham*—auspicious, and *bhu*—to be; hence it is equivalent to Shiva.

13) §. 15. Trilochana is 'three-eyed.' At Argos there long stood a three-eyed Zeus, a carved image, said to have been brought from Troy, having the third eye in the forehead and symbolising the Prehellenic combination in one god of the three kingdoms of the universe, afterwards divided among three divinities.—*Pausanias*, II. 24. 5. (Eng. transl. vol. I. pp. 189-90.)

14) §. 15. Among the other names and epithets of Shiva given in the *Amarakosha* (Book I. c. I. sec. 1. shl. 25-30) are—Pashupati—the lord of living creatures, whence a sect of his followers derive the name of *Páshupatas* (Colebrooke, *Essays*, vol. I. p. 406); Shúlin, Shúladhara—wielder of the trident; Sarva—who is all; 'Ishána; Chandrashékhara—whose crest is the moon; Khaṇḍaparshu—who hews his foes in pieces; Mṛiḍa—who is pleased; Mṛityuñjaya—the conqueror of death; Krittivásá—clothed with a hide; Pinákin—armed with the bow; Pramathádhipa—master of *Pramathas*; Ugra—the wrathful; Kapardin—of the braided hair; Shrikaṇṭha—of the beautiful throat; Shitikaṇṭha—of the black throat; Kapálabhṛit—whose alms-bowl is a skull; Vámadéva—who sports in a contrary way; Virúpáksha—having three eyes; Kṛishánuretas; Sarvadnya—the all-knowing; Dhurj-

jaṭi—who bears the three worlds; Nílalohita—the blue and red; Smarahara and Bharga—who killed the god of love; Tryambaka; Tripurántaka—the destroyer of the Asura named *Tripura*; Gaṅgádhara—who has the goddess *Gangá* in his hair; Andhakaripu—the enemy of *Andhaka;* Kratudhvansín—the destroyer of (*Daksha's*) sacrifice; Vṛishadhvaja—whose standard is a bull; Vyomakesha—azure haired; Bhava—the existing; Bhíma—the terrific; Stháṇú—the everlasting; and Umápati—the lord of *Umá.* Halayudha adds others as,—Ahirbundha—having his neck bound with a snake; Srashtṛi—the creator; Gaṇádhipa—leader of the *gaṇa*; Dakshádhvaradhvansakṛit—the overthrower of *Daksha's* sacrifice; Nílagríva —blue-necked; Paraméshvara—the best lord; Shipivishṭa; &c.

15) §. 15. Conf. Dr. J. Wilson, *Calcutta Rev.* vol. XLII. p. 11. The names of Párvatí given in the *Amarakosha* (Bk. I. c. i. sec. 1. shl. 32, 33.) are—

Umá, Kátyáyaní, Gaurí, Kálí, Haimavatí-shvarí,
Shivá, Bhaváni, Rudráni, Sarváni, Sarvamangalá,
Aparná, Párvatí, Durgá, Mṛiḍáni, Chaṇḍik-Ambiká,

Halayudha (I. 15, 16) adds Bhagávatí, Dákshayaní, Mahádeví, Girijá, Ménakátmajá, &c.

16) §. 16. Conf. Dr. Stevenson, *Jour. R. Asiat. Soc.* vol. VIII. p. 331; Lassen, *Alterthumskunde*, Bd. I. p. 783; Mr. Spiers, *Life in Ancient India*, pp. 374, 375.

17) §. 16. The worship of the Phallus formed a prominent part of the Osiris festival in Egypt. In Greece the emblem was a symbol of Hermes, especially in Arkadia; and at Kyllene in Elis he was long honoured only under the form of a simple phallus. Dionysos, the god of flocks, vines, and general productiveness, was worshipped at Sparta as Sukites, the fig-god, and at his feasts this symbol was always carried about in processions. Tertullian informs us that it was also exhibited in the Attic or Eleusinian mysteries, and Diodorus states that it was honoured in all the mysteries. In Italy it was also carried at the Liberalia in *Lavinium*, and was the common symbol of Priapus, who was supposed to bestow productiveness on flocks, fields, and gardens, and who in consequence was to be found in every garden and field daubed with vermilion, as such figures still are in India; and, as Mutinus-Tutunus or Fascinus, his image was prominent in the courts and even over the hearths of private houses. In the Dekhan and Konkan, Mhasoba corresponds best to Priapus as the god of the fields. Conf. Plutarch, *de Iside et Osiride* § 36, (Ed. Squire p. 90); Diodorus Siculus (ed Wesseling.) I. 22, and 88, and IV. 6; Jamblicus, I. 11, or Taylor's *transl.* pp. 51-55; Pausanias, VI. xxvi. 3; and ix. xxxi. 2; or Taylor's. *transl.* (Lond. 1826,) vol. II, p. 145, and vol. III. p. 63; Herodotus, II. 48, 49, and 51; Athenæus. lib. xiv. c. 56; Tertullian, *adv. Valent.* I.; Horat. *Sat.* I. viii. 1-7; Virgil, *Georg.* IV, 110, 111; Ovid, *Met.* IX. 347; *Fasti*, I. 391, 415; VI. 333, 345; Plin, *Hist. Nat.* XXVIII. iv. 7; Varro, *ap. Aug. C. D.* VII. 21; *August, C. D.* IV. 11 and VI. 9; Lucian, *de Syria Dea*, 16, 28, (ed. Hemsterh. et Gesneri, tom, III. pp. 463, 474); *Deor. dial.* xxiii, 1, (tom I. p. 273); and *de Saltat.* 21 (tom. II. p. 279); Gyrald. Ferrariensis, *Opera*, tom. I. pp. 262, 271, 280, 284; Stevenson, *Jour. R. As. Soc.* vol. VI. pp. 240, 241; Wilson, *Works*, vol. II. pp. 55, 63.

18) §. 16. See the Puránas of the Lingáyits, *Jour. Bomb. B. R. As. Soc.* vol. VIII. pp. 65-221, and *Madras Jour. Lit. and Sc. Soc.* vol. XII. pp. 271-292. They are also called. Víra-Shaivas or Jangamas, and carry a representation of the linga about their persons. The sect was founded by Basava, a Brahman of Kalyan in Karnata, about the middle of the twelfth century. They deny the sanctity of the Brahmanical order, and the authority of the Vedas, recognise various divinities, but virtually abolish the distinction of caste. See *Madras Jour. Lit. and Sc. Soc.* vol. XI. pp. 143-177; Wilson, *Works*, vol. I. pp. 219-230.

[19]) §. 16. Lassen is in error in asserting that no mention is made of the **L i n g a** in the *Mahabharata* or *Ramayana*. From the *Anushasana-parva* of the *Mahabharata*, Dr. J. Muir has cited the following (vv. 822 ff.) :—"Is 'Isha (*Mahadeva*) the cause of causes for any other reasons? We have not heard that the **l i n g a** of any other person is worshipped by the gods. Declare if thou hast heard what other being's **l i n g a** except that of **M a h e s h w a r a** is now worshipped, or has formerly been worshipped, by the gods? He whose **l i n g a B r a h m á** and **V i ṣ h ṇ u** and thou (*Indra*) with the deities, continually worship, is therefore the most eminent. Since children bear neither the mark of the lotus (*Brahma's*), nor of the discus (*Vishnu's*), nor of the thunderbolt (*Indra's*), but are marked with the male and female organs,—therefore offspring is derived from **M a h e s h w a r a**. All women produced from the nature of **D e v í** as their cause, are marked with the female organ, and all males are manifestly marked with the **l i n g a** of **H a r a**." And again, (v. 7510,) "And since, standing aloft he consumes the lives of men, and since he is fixed, and since his **l i n g a** is perpetually fixed, he is therefore called **S t h á ṇ ú**.........(7516) and when his **l i n g a** remains constantly in a state of chastity, and people reverence it, this is agreeable to the great [god]. The constant worshipper of the **l i n g a**, who shall worship the image (*vigraha*), or the **l i n g a** of the great [god], enjoys great prosperity. It is the **l i n g a**, raised up, which the rishis, gods, Gandharvas, and Apsarases worship." And once more, in the list of Shiva's names v. 1160 :—"He whose seed is raised up, whose **l i n g a** is raised up, who sleeps aloft, who abides in the sky".........1191. "The lord of the **l i n g a**, the lord of the **s u r a s** (gods)......the lord of seed, the former of seed." And in the *Uttara Kanda* of the *Ramayana*, (36, v. 42f.), we have "Wherever **R á v a ṇ a**, lord of the **R á k s h a s a s**, went, a golden **l i n g a** was carried thither. Placing that **l i n g a** in the midst of a pedestal of sand, **R á v a n a** worshipped it with incense and flowers of ambrosial odour."—Muir, *Sansk. Texts*, Pt. IV. pp. 161, 344, 421.

[20]) §. 16. Conf. §. 63, and the story from the *Vayu Purana* in Wilson's *Vishnu Purana* (4to. ed.) pp. 61-69; or (8vo. ed.) vol. I. pp. 120-134.

[21]). §. 16. See Muir, *Original Sanskrit Texts*, Pt. IV. pp. 325-330 ; and *Channabasava Purana*, in *Jour. Bomb. Br. R. As. Soc.* Vol. VIII. pp. 142-144 ; Vans Kennedy, *Hindu Mythology*, pp. 271-273.

[22]) §. 16. *Channabasava Purana*, ut sup. p. 145 ; *Skanda Purana* in Vans Kennedy, *ut. sup.* p. 275-277 ; Ward, *Hist. Liter. and Religion of the Hindus*, Vol. I. p. 35. ; Paterson, *Asiat. Res.* Vol. VIII. p. 49 ; A. Roger, *La Porte Ouverte* (Amsterdam 1670), p. 144, &c. The majority of the accounts represent the destruction of **B r a h m á**'s head as the punishment of his pride.

[23]) §. 17. Griffiths, *Birth of the War-God*, Canto V. pp. 52, 53.

[24]) §. 18. *Jour. Bomb. B. R. As. Soc.* vol. IV. pp. 270-71. Of the **S m á r t t a B r a h m a n s** of Southern India, Buchanan says :—"The most numerous class here and which comprehends about one half of all the Brahmans of the Lower Karnatak, is called the **S m á r t t a** sect, and its members are the followers of **S h a n k a r a 'A c h á r y a**. They are commonly said to be of the sect of **S h i v a**, but they consider **B r a h m á**, **V i ṣ h ṇ u**, and **'I s h v a r a** to be the same as the creator, preserver, and destroyer of the universe. They are readily distinguished by three horizontal stripes on the forehead, made with the ashes of cowdung." *Journey through Mysore*, &c., vol. I. pp. 13, 14, see also pp. 304-305.

[25]) §. 18. De Couto, *Da Asia*, Dec. VII. liv. iii. cap. 11., tom. VII. p. 259.

[26]) §. 18. De Couto, ut. sup. pp. 260-61. He adds that **U q u á** (**O k h á** or **U s h á**) a daughter of **B á n á s u r a**, who dedicated herself in this temple to perpetual virginity, lived here for many years ; and that "the ancients say that in the time of king **B á n á s u r a**

gold rained at Elephanta for three hours, and it was therefore called Santupori (*Shonitapura*), that is to say, in their language, the Isle of Gold." For the story of Bánásura and his daughter Ushá, who fell in love with Aniruddha, the son of Pradyumna and grandson of Krishna, see Wilson, *Vishnu Purana*, Book V. ch. 32 and 33; (4to ed.) pp. 591-96; *Narmakathakosha*, s. v. 'Ushá,' &c; Ward, *Hindus*, vol. I. p. 26; and Wilson, *Hindu Theatre*, vol. II. pp. 396-99. Conf. *Archæologia*, vol. VII. p. 328; Grose, *Voyage*, vol. I. p. 61; and *Asiat. Res.* vol. IV. p. 415.

27) §. 18. *Jour. Bomb. B. R. As. Soc.* vol. IV. p. 262. Speaking of the Dumar Lena Cave at Elura, Mr. Fergusson says—"This temple with the one at Elephanta, if I am correct in the views I have stated above, must have been executed in the tenth century of our era, a date which I do not think can possibly be far from the truth." Dr. Wilson says—"Somewhat posterior, in point of age, to Kailása must be those Brahmanical temples of Elephanta and Salsette, in which various imitations of the Brahmanical excavations of Elorá appear. Looking at them collectively, we have long, on mythological grounds, been disposed to limit the age of the Brahmanical excavated temples to the eighth or ninth century after Christ. On several of their figures the small box, containing the emblem of Shiva, worn by the Lingáyits is represented, and the Lingáyits did not appear in the south of India till considerable modifications were made, in the course of time, in the peculiar forms of Shaivism introduced or supported by Shankara 'Acharya. The Cholá rájas were the patrons of the Lingáyits, who, to the worship of Mahádeva or Shiva, added the practice of Yoga, without reference to caste, with a view to final emancipation. Professor Wilson (*Asiat. Res.* vol. XVII. p. 188) notices the profession of the Yoga in the eighth century, and he properly observes that the Brahmanical temples in the subjects of their sculptures, and the decorations of Shiva and his attendants, belong to the same sect. It is remarkable that this form of the Hindu religion has vanished from the Maráthá country, which it is not likely that it would have done had it enjoyed the continued patronage of the Devagiri Rájás reigning over this [Elorá] locality, the last of whom was overcome by the Muhammadans A.D. 1293." In his Second Memoir, the Doctor adds,—"When examining the Jaina excavation of Párasnátha, which is of the same workmanship as the larger Jaina excavations, we discovered an original inscription, a small portion of which in an incorrect form had been furnished to Dr. Bird, giving the date of its formation as Shaka 1156, equivalent to about A. D. 1234, which makes the Jaina temples at Elorá 618 years old at the present time [1852]. In the inscription referred to the name of the hill in which the Elorá excavations are made is the Virollá Parvata, or mount of Virollá. This word, we have little doubt, is formed from the name of Vira-Cholá, one the Cholá Rajas, who flourished, according to one of the papers of the Mackenzie collection, quoted by Professor H. H. Wilson (who mentions the extensive conquests of his race), about A.D. 917. This gives an antiquity to the most remarkable of the BRAHMANICAL temples of Elorá and those of Elephanta, which are of the same type, of about 935 years; or, to deal in round numbers, it makes them to fall at least within the present millennium." It must be allowed that this argument is rather loose, so far as fixing the age of the 'Dumar Lena' cave is concerned. That cave is probably older than Kailása, and perhaps not quite so old as Elephanta. The badge of the Lingayits is not found at Elephanta. Fergusson, *Rock-Cut Temples*, p. 52; Dr. J. Wilson, *Jour. Bomb. B. R. As. Soc.* vol. III. Pt. II. pp. 83, 84; vol. IV. p. 369; and *Calcutta Rev.* vol. XLII. pp. 16, 17. See below note 38.

28) §. 20. Sir W. Jones, *Asiat. Res.* vol. I. p. 273; Philippsohn, *Development of the Religious Idea* [Lond. 1855], p. 156; Hardwick, *Christ and other Masters*, vol. I. pp. 174, 198, 199, and 275; Vans Kennedy, *Researches in Hindu Mythology*, pp. 211, 212.

29) §. 21. Erskine, *Trans. Lit. Soc. Bomb.* vol. III. p. 524; and Sykes, *Jour. R. Asiat. Soc.* vol. V. pp. 81, 83.

30) §. 21. *Birth of War-God*, p. 73.

31) §. 21. There can be little doubt but the apparently feminine traits were given to the Vishṇu face of the Trimurti to express the character of kindliness or complacency appropriate to the Preserver; and it is not improbable that a re-examination of the busts at Elura from which Col. Sykes inferred that the third was that of Párvatí, might lead to a different conclusion from the one he arrived at and in which Erskine concurred. The following extracts from the *Puranas* will show how unanimously they agree as to the persons and functions of the members of the Triad:—The *Vayu Purana* (ch. V. vv. 11-21) says:—"At the beginning of the day, the supreme lord Maheshwara sprung from Prakṛiti, entering the egg, agitated with extreme intentness both Pradhána (=Prakṛiti—matter) and Purusha [spirit]. From Pradhána, when agitated, the quality of passion (*rajas*) arose, which was there a stimulating cause, as water is in seeds. When an inequality in the Guṇas arises, then (the deities) who preside over them are generated. From the Guṇas thus agitated there sprang three gods, indwelling, supreme, mysterious, animating all things, embodied. The *rajas* quality was born as Brahmá, the *tamas* as Agni,—the *sattva* as Vishṇu. [The *Márkandeya Purana* ch. xlvi. v. 18. has the same line, but substitutes Rudra for Agni.] Brahmá, the manifester of *rajas*, acts in the character of creator; Agni, the manifester of *tamas*, acts in the capacity of time (kála); Vishṇu, the manifester of *sattva*, abides in a condition of indifference. These deities are the three worlds, the three Vedas, the three fires; they are mutually dependent, mutually devoted. They exist through each other, and uphold each other; they are twin-parts of one another, they subsist through one another. They are not for a moment separated; they never abandon one another. Ishwara is the supreme god; and Vishṇu is superior to *Mahat*, (the principle of intelligence); while Brahmá, filled with *rajas*, engages in creation. Purusha is to be regarded as supreme, as Prakṛiti is also declared to be."

The *Linga Purana* begins with the line—"Adored be Rudra, Hari (*Vishnu*), and Brahmá the supreme spirit," and in the commencement of the 11th Adhyayá we have a short account of the manifestation of Shiva as Purusha and Prakriti, and then of the Linga as one, seven, eight, and eleven, and in the 6th shloka we are told,—"after the chief of all the gods, the Triad manifestation of Shiva was produced. The world sprung from one of these three, by another it is preserved, and by a third it is destroyed, and the whole world is preserved by this one Shiva." Again (*Linga Purana*, Part I. 3. 28ff.) we read:—"These principles from *Mahat* to the gross elements inclusive, generate an egg, like a bubble of water, from which issued (Pitámaha) the Parent [of the universe] who was the same as the divine Rudra and Vishṇu, the omnipresent lord. Within that egg were these worlds—this entire universe.........its soul is Kamalásana (*Brahma*)." And (Pt. I. 17.)—"Pitámaha (*Brahma*) says: Pradhána (nature) is called the Linga, and Parameshvara is called Lingí (the sustainer of the Linga).........When the Vaimánika creation had proceeded with the rishis to Janaloka, and when—the period of the continuance [of the world] having been completed,—[all things] had been absorbed.........and all immoveable things having become altogether dried up from want of rain,—beasts, men, trees, Pisháchas, flesh-eating goblins, Gandharvas, &c. were by degrees burnt up by the rays of the sun. The one awful ocean being everywhere enveloped in darkness, the great-armed Náráyaṇa, the soul of all things, formed of existence and non-existence, sleeps upon the water, plunged in contemplation, spotless, tranquil, thousand-headed, the soul of the universe, thousand-eyed, thousand-footed, thousand-armed, omniscient, the source of all the gods, he who is himself through passion (*rajas*) Hiranyagarbha

[*Brahmá*], through darkness (*tamas*) Shankara, through goodness (*sattva*) the all-pervading Vishṇu, and in his universality Maheshvara, having the character of time, the name of time [*Kála*], white, black, free from the three qualities." And yet again (I. 18.)—"I (Vishvesha or Mahádeva), the undivided supreme lord, am divided in a threefold manner under the names of Brahmá, Vishṇu, and Bhava, possessing the attributes of creating, preserving, and destroying." Lastly (I. 68) we read :—" At the time of creation this god (Shiva) issued from the mundane egg in a corporeal form resplendent as the sun; and then sprang from his left side Vishṇu, the adored by men and gods, and Lakshmí; and from his right side Brahmá and Sarasvatí ...... And as there are three Vedas, three qualities, three worlds, and three fires, so are there three gods who depend upon and assist each other, and, together mutually subsisting and acting, are never for a moment disunited. Shiva is the supreme god; Vishṇu also is supremely eminent; and Brahmá being united to the quality of impurity, is the creator of all things. At the beginning of time, by the will of Ishwara, the cause of entity and nonentity, the three qualities becoming disproportionately combined, visibility was produced from invisibility, and the powers of Vishṇu and Brahmá for framing and preserving this universe were originated. Thus there is but one Supreme being, though assuming three forms."

In the *Patala Khanda* of the *Padma Purana*, chapter entitled *Bhasmopatti vidhanam*, we read,—" That eternal, imperishable, incorporeal, and supreme god, Shiva, though exempt from quality, yet being desirous of creation, assumed the three qualities, and then separated from his spiritual essence three hypostases. From his right side proceeded Brahmá, from his left Vishṇu, and from his back Rudra; and thus did that god produce three sons." The *Kurma Purana* (pt. I. c. 4) says,—The mundane egg " was the first form under which the Supreme being manifested himself; the next was that of Hiranyagarbha, who issued from that golden egg; then, for the purpose of delivering the Vedas and creating the universe, he united himself to the quality of impurity, and appeared as the four-faced Brahmá; to preserve, likewise, these worlds, he has combined himself with the quality of purity, and assumed the form of Vishṇu; and at the end of time will that supreme being, uniting himself to the quality of darkness, under the character of Rudra, destroy this universe. Thus there is but one omnipotent god, who, though devoid of affection and quality, yet invests himself with the three qualities, and appears under three forms, for the purposes of creation, preservation, and destruction." So in the *Naradiya Purana* (c. 3) :—" Then, for the purposes of creating, did he produce Brahmá from his right side; of destroying Rudrá from his middle; and of preserving Vishṇu from his left side; and the supreme being, having thus at the beginning of time, assumed three forms, is sometimes called Brahmá, sometimes Vishṇu, and sometimes Shiva............Purushá, Prakriti, and Kála, [the active and passive powers of Nature and Time] are the threefold causes of creation, preservation, and destruction. Their complete union is the form of Parabrahm; and, when disunited, a god receives his name from each : for he who creates, is called Brahmá; who preserves, Vishṇu; and who destroys, Shiva." And in the *Suta Sanhita* of the *Skanda Purana* (*Yadnya-vaibhava*, c. 6.)—" Rudra, however, and Vishṇu and Brahmá sometimes render themselves manifest; but knowledge convinces us that these are merely three forms of one supreme being ...... Through his favour alone it is that by the manifestation of other gods we are enabled to comprehend his essence ...... As, therefore, those three forms are his efficient agents, let us always with delight devoutly meditate on the celestial figures of Rudrá, Vishṇu, and Brahmá; who when they proceeded from his essence, were not subjected to the accidents of this life; yet are not these three gods equal to Shiva, and whoever shall consider them as such shall visit the regions of hell."

In the *Uttara Khanda* of the *Shiva Purana*, Shiva is invoked thus: ' Hail to Shambhu whose right side produced Vágísha (Brahmá, the lord of speech), and his left Viṣhṇu; from whose arms proceeded the Vedas; who is celebrated by the faithful Munis chaunting the Sámavedas. Hail to that god whose form is unknown to Indra and the other gods, or to the sons of Dití, to the demons, and who is the creator, the preserver, and the destroyer of the universe?"

Colebrooke thus summarizes the Hindu doctrine on the relation of these three divinities and their connection with the creation: "This universe," he says, "consisting of three worlds, was produced from water. 'He first, with a thought, created the waters, and placed in them a productive seed.' (*Menu.* chap. I. v. 8.) Water, which is the element whence the three worlds proceeded, is that light which is also the efficient cause of creation, duration, and destruction, manifested with these powers, in the form of Brahmá, Viṣhṇu, and Rudra: to denote this, 'earth, sky, and heaven,' are subjoined as epithets of light. These terms bear allusion also to the three qualities of truth, passion, and darkness, corresponding with the three manifestations of power, as creator, preserver, and destroyer; hence it is also intimated, that the irradiating being is manifested as Brahmá, Viṣhṇu, and Rudrá, who are respectively endued with the qualities of truth, passion, and darkness. The meaning is, that this irradiating being, who is the the supreme Brahme manifested in three forms or powers, is the efficient cause of the creation of the universe, of its duration and destruction."

Finally Prof. H. H. Wilson remarks of this Trimurti:—"There can be little doubt that it is, as Mr. Erskine supposes, the bust of Shiva alone, although possibly the other two heads may express Brahmá and Viṣhṇu, as one with Shiva. More correctly still, however, we may consider it to be Shiva, invested with the triple character of creator, preserver, and destroyer—an aggregation of attributes always assigned by the sectarian Hindu to the divinity of his preferential adoration. Muir, *Original Sansk. Texts*, vol. I. pp. 74, 75; vol. IV. pp. 36, 327, 330; Stevenson, *Jour. Bomb. B. R. As. Soc.* vol IV. p. 271; Vans Kennedy, *Researches into Hindu Mythology*, pp. 200-206; Colebrooke, *Essays*, vol. I. pp. 131, 132; Wilson, *Quart. Oriental Mag.* (Calcutta, 1824) p. 11.

Major E. Moor discovered two images of the Trímurti among the ruins of a temple at Walakeshwar on Malabar hill, figured in his *Hindu Pantheon*, plates 81, 82.

32) § 22. "Brahmá," says the *Mundaka Upanishad*, "was produced the first among the gods, maker of the universe, preserver of the world."—Muir, *Orig. Sansk. Texts.* vol. III. p. 31. In preceding quotations from the *Puranas*, it will be observed that he is frequently spoken of as the *Creator*; this epithet, however, Vans Kennedy considers to be misapplied to Brahmá "because no act of creation is ever ascribed to him,......... Brahmá, therefore is invariably represented as being only the producer or progenitor of all classes of animated beings."—*Researches in Hindu Mythology*, p. 270.

33) §. 22. From Prof. H. H. Wilson's Review of Mr. Erskine's paper, the following remarks may be here quoted:—"It is noticed by Mr. Erskine," he says, "that the ears of the Central head are elongated like those of the Kánpáthes (*Kanphata Yogis*); and in like manner they are embellished with ponderous ear-rings. We have already noticed the appearance of this sect in the caves of Salsette, and we again trace them at Elephanta: it is not unlikely therefore that they are the architects of these excavations. They are a meditative and monastic race who worship Shiva especially; they are an antient order, and have now almost disappeared, being represented by a few vagabond mendicants who assume the name of Kánphátás, and as the term denotes, have their ears split or pierced, wearing heavy rings in the perforation. The only respectable establishment of Yogis known in this part of India is one near Gorakhpura, a temple and establishment sacred to Shiva as Gorakhnátha or Gorakshanátha.

The same form of S h i v a and other analogous ones have many temples in Nepal ; but neither Kirkpatrick nor Hamilton mention *Yogis :* and although therefore the temples which are of considerable antiquity, remain, the sect must have declined there also, if not have disappeared. Admitting that the cavern temples of the S h i v a faith were constructed by the Y o g i s : a deduction of some importance immediately follows. We need not be surprised to meet with figures and subjects to which the legendary history of the Hindus, as far as yet investigated, furnishes no clue. Beyond the object and act of Y o g a, which are explained in the *Puranas*, and some of the philosophical systems, we are wholly unacquainted with the doctrines and practices of the Y o g i s : and their peculiarities, of course, are founded on legends known only to their system or on peculiar modifications of those common to the Hindu mythology. It is therefore necessary to make ourselves acquainted with this branch of Hindu literature, before we can hope to explain, in a manner wholly satisfactory, all the sculptures of Elephanta or similar excavations."—*Oriental Mag*. 1824, p. 11 ; and conf. *Essays*, vol. I. pp. 212-13, 216-18 ; Postans, *Jour. R. Asiat. Soc.* vol. V. pp. 268-71.

34) §. 22. *Trans. Lit. Soc. Bomb.* vol. I. p. 217.

35) §. 23. V i r a b h a d r a, an avatára of S h i v a, and K á l í—a form of his consort, are often represented with such tusks. Conf. Moor, *Hindu Pantheon*, plates 26, 28.

36) §. 26. " In the Hindu mythology, B r a h m á is represented of a red, V i s h ṇ u of a black or dark azure, and H a r a of a white complexion."—Moor, *Hind. Panth.* pp. 44, 97.

37) §. 26 Erskine adds the following dimensions:—The distance from the little finger of the right-hand figure to that of the left-hand figure is 15 feet 4 inches. The middle figure from ear to ear measures 6 feet 10½ inches ; from the top of the nose to the bottom of the chin 3 feet 2 inches ; the length of the nose is 1 foot 7½ inches ; distance between the further corners of the eyes 3 feet 10 inches ; from the wristlet to the point of the finger of the right-hand figure is 7 feet 10 inches. The right hand figure from the top of the nose to the bottom of the chin measures 3 feet 7 inches ; distance between the outer corners of the two eyes 4 feet 2 inches. The left-hand figure from the top of the nose to the bottom of the chin, 2 feet 11 inches ; exterior corners of the eyes, 4 feet 3 inches.—*Trans. Bom. Lit. Soc.* vol. I. p. 214, note.

38). §. 27. Dr. J. Wilson, *Calc. Rev.*, vol. XLII. p. 12.

39). §. 27. *Archæologia*, vol. VIII. pp. 270-71. Dr. Hunter in 1784 similarly remarks :—" The figures have suffered nothing from time, for the surfaces of them all are smooth and well defined ; but all the mutilations which they have sustained proceed from the brutal violence of barbarians who delight in mischief and are enemies to taste and science."—*Archæologia*, vol. VII. p. 295. So also Stevenson, *Jour. Bom. B. R. As. Soc.* vol. IV. p. 262 ; Moor. *Hind. Panth.* pp. 249, 334-35. Capt. Grindlay (1828) mentions an arm of one of the large figures in Elephánta in the possession of Sir Charles Forbes, Bart., M.P. How he obtained it we are left to conjecture.—*Trans. R. Asiat. Soc.* vol. II. p. 327.

40) §. 28. Niebuhr's plate represents it intact ; and even in Erskine's, the left arm is entire or nearly so.

41) §. 28. The P i s h á c h a s are the usual attendants and messengers of S h i v a and his wife P á r v a t í, and were created by him in his *avatara* of R u d r a ; their favourite residence is in burning or burying grounds, where S h i v a also delights to dwell ; they are his favourite g a ṇ a or retinue, whence his name of B h ú t p a t i or ' lord of demons.'—Erskine, *Trans. Bom. Lit Soc.* vol. I. pp. 219-20.

42) §. 28. The fingers of this figure have disappeared since Erskine's time.

43) §. 28. It is represented entire in Niebuhr's plate V.

44) §. 29. Erskine mentions that in 1813, a large fragment broken off this figure " from the belly downwards, including the thighs and legs" lay on the ground.—*Trans. Bomb. Lit. Soc.* vol. I. p. 219.

45) §. 29. The head dresses of two male figures in one of the chapels of Cave II. at Ajaṇṭá, bear a strong resemblance to what we find here.

46) §. 29. Erskine ut. sup. p. 219, and Niebuhr's Plate V. Erskine speaks of the neck of this dwárapála and of the central head of the Trimurti as "rising in folds": —a careful examination of the different figures where this feature occurs, shows that the 'folds' belong to the band that fastens the mukuta on the head.

47) §. 31. *Archæologia* vol. VII. p. 289.

48) §. 35. Erskine, *ut. sup.* p. 239.

49) §. 35. "The pedestal (*vedi*) of the Linga is Mahádeví (Umá) and the Linga is the visible Maheshwara"—*Linga Purana*, I. 18. in Muir, *Sansk. Texts*, Pt. IV. p. 330. The *vedi* itself is commonly known as chavaraṇga, and the linga as pindi.

50) §. 36. This is called áchamana. The 'god and goddess of learning' invoked with Gaṇesha, are Guru and Sarasvati: The usual mantra is—" To obtain success in all undertakings, I first salute Vináyaka (Gaṇesha), Guru, Bhánu (the sun), Brahmá, Vishnu, Maheshwara, and Sarasvatí."

51) §. 36. This is called áváhana.

52) §. 36. This is called pádya—water for cleansing the feet; from páda the foot.

53) §. 36. The bathing with water is called snána, and with the five others panchámṛitasnána. After these washings the Gujaratis press their eyes with their wet fingers, performing nirmála vandana.

54) §. 36. Essential parts of these mantras are the various names of Rudra. The bell is also rung after the *abhisheka* or bathing. Much of the detail of the account of the ritual in the text is due to Mr. Krishna Shastri Godbole.

55) §. 37. De Couto, *Da Asia*, ut. sup. p. 254.

56) §. 38. Conf. Linschoten, ut. sup.; De Couto, ut. sup. p. 258; Niebuhr, *Voy.* tom. II. p. 27.; Hunter, *Archæologia*, vol. VII. p. 293; Macneil, ib. vol. VIII. p. 274; and Goldingham, *Asiat. Res.* vol. IV. p. 410. Ouseley (*Travels*, vol. I. p. 83) supposed the left breast had been broken off.

57) §. 38. This figure is also called Arddhanárínaṭeshvara. The idea of a divinity half-male and half-female is of considerable antiquity. In the *Purusha Sukta* —*Rig Veda*, X. 90, we read,—" From him (*Purusha*) was born Viráj and from Viráj, Purusha" and in the *Bṛihadaraṇyaka* of the *Shatapatha Brahmana*—" He (*Viraj*— the primeval and universal manifested being) wished [*the existence of*] another; and instantly he became such as is man and woman in mutual embrace. He caused this his own self to fall in twain; and thus became a husband and a wife." And in *Manu's Institutes* (I. 32) " Having divided his own body into two parts, the lord (*Brahma*) became with the half a male (*purusha*) and with the half a female; and in her he created Viráj. Know O most excellent twice-born men that I, whom that male (*purusha*) Viráj, himself created, am the creator of all this world." A still clearer statement connected with Arddhanáríshvara is quoted in §. 43. In the *Kalika Purana* it is said— " Hara offered his wife to take half of her body and to give her half of his own, or *vice versa*; and at length she took the half of Shiva and joined it to her right side, and the god took half of Párvatí and united it to his. Thus forming only one body with his wife, Shiva has the name of Arddhanáríshvara."

In the opening invocation of the *Raghuvansa*, Kalidása addresses **Shiva** and his consort as united like *word* and *sense* or *meaning* :—

" The pair like thought and speech conjoined (that I may thought and speech obtain.)
The world's great parents I invoke,—Párvati and the Lord supreme."

In the *Vishnu Purana* (I. 7. 6-13) we are told—" Sanandana and the other sons who had been previously created by Vedhas (Brahmá) had no regard for the worlds, and were undesirous of offspring. They had all attained to knowledge, were free from desire, and devoid of envy. As they were thus indifferent about the creation of the world, great wrath sufficient to burn up the three worlds, arose in the mighty Brahmá. The three worlds became quite illuminated in every part by the wreath of flame that sprung from his anger. Then from his forehead, wrinkled by frowns and inflamed by fury, arose Rudra, luminous as the mid-day sun, with a body half male and half female, fierce and huge in bulk. After saying to him, 'Divide thyself,' Brahmá vanished. Being so addressed, Rudra severed himself into two, into a male and a female form."

In the *Channabasava Purana* of the Lingayits, we have this other account : —" Brahmá commenced his work (the creation); but it did not succeed on account of his former falsehood. He pleased Shiva by many penances, and prayed to him to become his son, because he was unable to create the world without his assistance. Shiva answered him, saying: 'But in that case you will not survive. Fool! Ask with discretion!' Nevertheless he insisted on it. According to Brahmá's prayer Mahesha with Umáshakti issued from his forehead, whereby the body of the former was split into two pieces. Mahesha then took the terrific form of Rudra, and Umá the horrid figure of **Mahákálí**. When Brahmá, whose body Shiva had again joined together and made alive, saw this horrible form, he prayed to him to take another and a single form. Complying with this request, Shiva united Mahákálí with his own body in one, and thus became **Arddhanárishvara**." The account given in the *Linga Purana* runs thus :—After their marriage Shiva and Párvatí lived on Mount Kailása, where Párvatí kept house, and Shiva supported the family as a mendicant. One day Shiva having smoked intoxicating herbs to excess, was unable to go his daily rounds. Párvati informed him that there was nothing in the house; as the family had eaten half the alms collected the day before, and Gaṇesha's rat and Kárttikéya's peacock had devoured the rest. After much altercation, Shiva left the hut to beg, and his wife went off to her father's to obtain food taking her children with her. On the way she met Nárada, who advised her to assume the form of Anna-purna (the goddess of food) and to lay an embargo on all the food at the houses where Shiva would beg. She did so, and Shiva begged in vain for a handful of rice. Nárada met Shiva also and advised him to go back to his wife: Párvati received him with delight and satisfied his hunger; which so pleased the old beggar that he pressed her in his arms until both bodies became one.—Still more childish stories are told in the later *tantrika* works.

This union of Shiva and Párvatí in a single body personifies the principle of life and production in its double aspect—the active principle under the name of Purusha, and the passive under that of Prakṛiti. It embodies the central idea of nature-worship; and seems to have occurred to the early Greeks as well as to the Hindus as we may infer from the old Orphic hymn preserved by Stobæus :—

Ζεὺς ἄρσην γένετο, Ζεὺς ἄμβροτος ἔπλετο νύμφη.

" Zeus was a male, Zeus became a deathless damsel."

The figure of Arddhanárinaṭeshwara is usually painted dark blue or black on the male side, and vermilion or orange on the left or female side, but sometimes the colours are white and yellow. Conf. Muir, *Orig. Sansk. Texts.* vol. I. pp. 9 and 36 ; IV. p. 331 ; and V. p. 369 ; *Jour. R. As. Soc.* 1865, p. 354 ; Colebrooke, *Essays*, vol. I. pp. 62, 64 ; *Raghuvansa*, ed. Stenzler, p. 1 ; and *Jour. Bom. B. R. As. Soc.* vol. I. p. 315 ; vol. VIII. p. 144 ; Wilson, *Vishnu Pur.* (4to. ed.) pp. 49-51, (8vo. ed.) vol I. pp. 100-104 ; Stobæus, *Ecl. Phys.*, ed. Heeren, vol. I. p. 42 ; Moor, *Hindu Pantheon*, p. 80 ; H. H. Wilson, *Works*, vol. III. p. 212 ; Ward, *Hindus*, vol. I. p. 239 ; D'Hancarville, *Recherches sur l'Origine, &c. des Arts de la Grece*, tom. I. p. 77 ; Sir W. Ouseley, *Travels*, vol. I. p. 83 ; Mill and Wilson, *Hist. Ind.* vol. I. p. 369 ; Maurice, *Indian Antiquities*, vol. V. p. 933.

58) §. 38. Some of the expressions in the text are somewhat free renderings, but the fragment referred to of *Porphyry's* lost treatise *de Styge*, is perhaps of sufficient interest to deserve the insertion here of a translation of the whole passage as given by *Stobæus*, Lib. I. cap. iv. §. 56. (ed. Heeren, vol. I. pp. 140-152) :—

The Indians, who in the reign of *Antoninus of Emesa* [*Elagabalus*] came to speech in Syria with *Bardisanes* the Mesopotamian, told him, as he has recorded, that the Indians then still had a lake called the Lake of Trial, and that, if any Indian denied a crime imputed to him, [he went down] into this lake [to be tried]. Now some of the *Brachmanes* try him in this fashion : They ask the man if he wishes the proof to be by the water ; and if he is not willing, they send him off to pay the penalty, as answerable for the crime : but if he accepts the test, they put him in with his accusers : for these too go down into the water, to be tried whether they give false evidence. Those then who enter the water pass through to the other side of the lake. Now, the depth is up to the knees of any man whomsoever entering the lake. When then the accused man enters; if he be innocent, he fearlessly passes through with the water up to his knees : but if he be guilty, after going on a little way, he sinks up to his head. But the *Brachmanes* pull him out of the water, deliver him alive to those that bring him (his accusers), and order him to be punished, the penalty of death excepted. Now they say that this test is seldom used, as no man dares to deny his sin because of the trial by the water. For voluntary sins then the Indians have this water as a test : while for involuntary as well as voluntary sins, and generally for a correct life, there is another water. And about this other Bardisanes writes as follows, for I will tell his story in his own words : " Now they said that there was also a natural and vast cave in a very lofty mountain nearly " about the middle of the land. And in this cave there is a statue, which they guess to be " of ten or twelve cubits. It stands upright with the hands extended in the form of a cross. " And the right of its face is that of a man, while the left is that of a woman. Now in the " same way the right arm too and the right foot and the whole half are of a man, and the " left of a woman : so that on seeing it we are astonished that we can see the dissimilarity " of two sides in one body without division. In this statue they say are carved round the " right breast the sun, round the left the moon ; and down the two arms are cleverly carved " a number of angels and all things that exist in the universe ; that is, the heaven, and " mountains, and the sea, and the river of ocean, and plants, and animals, and in a word all " things that are. This statue they say God gave his son what time he was creating the " universe, that he might have a visible model. Now I asked," says *Bardisanes*, " of what " substance the statue was. And *Sandales* declared, whilst the others also bore him " out, that no man knew of what substance that statue was ; for it was not of gold, nor " silver, nor bronze, nor stone, nor other substance, but rather was like very solid and " imperishable wood, and yet was not wood. Now they said further, that a certain king " wished to pluck out one hair of those round the neck of the statue, and blood flowed, and " that king was affrighted so that he hardly revived through the prayers of the *Brach-* " *manes*. Now upon the head of the statue they say is an image of a god, seated as it were " upon a throne. But they say also that in the summer heats the whole of this statue "sweats, and that it is fanned by the *Brachmanes* and the sweats cease; and if they do not "fan, it gives out much sweat so that the ground round it is wet. But at a great distance "beyond the statue there is darkness in the cave: and there those who please go in "with torches and find an opening, from which water flows forth forming a pool round "the end of the cave. And men, as trying themselves, enter through that opening. And "all who are pure from vices of life, enter without hindrance as the opening becomes "wider, and find a very great spring of water very clear and very sweet and from this "spring the water aforesaid flows forth. But those who are conscious of guilt press much to "pass in through that opening, and cannot, for it becomes narrow. All of these are forced to "confess before the rest if they have done any wrong, and they beg the others to pray for "them and they fast for a long time. To this place, but on a fixed day," says *Bardisanes*, "the men with *Sandales* declared the *Brachmanes* gather. But some of them pass their "lives there, whilst others in the summer time and about autumn, when fruit is abundant, "gather together from other places to see the statue and meet one another, and make "trial of themselves if they can pass through the aforesaid opening. Now the people there "they say are making inquiries about the carving on that figure; for it is not easy to under-"stand the whole imagery, both because there are many things, and because all the "animals and plants do not exist in every country. This then is the story the Indians tell "about the Water of Trial which they have. But I think that *Apollonius* of *Tyana* also "remembered this,—I mean the water in the cave; for, writing to the *Brachmanes*, he swears "by an oath; 'nay, by the water of Tantalus in which you initiated me.' For I think he "calls this the *water of Tantalus*, because it ever punishes by expectation those who en-"deavour to come to it and to take a draught of it."

This is the report of a conversation between *Bardisanes* and men whose language he probably understood very imperfectly, and whose statements, even if literally rendered, were not perhaps specially calculated to convey strictly accurate ideas to the mind of a foreigner; but if we make allowance for this, the account of the statue is easily reconcilable with that of A r d d h a n á r í. And the 'opening' he refers to as a test of innocence, must at once recal the hole in the rock at *Malabar Point* or Wálakéshwar, to which, even in modern times, 'numerous pilgrims used to resort for the purpose of regeneration by the efficacy of a passage through it.' The mention, in the third century, of two such objects of religious import, found in a later age in such close local proximity is somewhat remarkable. See Moor, *Hind. Panth.* p. 395.

69) §. 38. From the crescent moon worn by S h i v a, he derives several names as C h a n-d r a m a u l i and C h a n d r a s h é k h a r a—moon crested, C h a n d r á p i d a—with the moon chaplet, C h a n d r i l a—bright as the moon, and S u d h á s ú t i k a l á m a u l i n,—having the nectar-producing crescent as a crest. The Moon is called S u d h á s ú t i—the producer of nectar, S u d h á k a r a—the nectar mine, S u d h á d h á r a and S u d h á n a d h i—the receptacle of nectar, S u d h á b h ṛ i t i—the nectar cherisher, S u d h á n g a—whose substance is nectar, and S u d h á n s h u—nectar-rayed. It is fabled that the full moon is filled with the drink of immortality, and that she wanes as the gods drink it up. "It is replenished," says the *Vayu Purana*, "from the sun during the fortnight of increase. On the full moon the gods adore that planet for one night, and from the first day, all of them, together with the p i t ṛ i s and ṛ i s h i s, drink one k a l á or digit daily until the ambrosia is exhausted." The moon is frequently alluded to by the poets as the receptacle of *Amrita*. Thus, in *Vikramorvasi*, the celestial nymph is represented saying—

"Delightful words! they fall like drops of nectar.
Nor wonder nectar from the moon should flow."

Wilson, *Hind. Theat.* vol. I. pp. 22, 202, and compare Wilson, *Essays on Sansk. Lit.* vol. II.

p. 389; the quotation from '*Malatimadhava*' in §. 62; and note 88. Garuḍa went to the moon to steal the nectar, and to make sure of it he tried to seize and hide the whole moon under his wings.—See the *Astika-Sauparnaparva* of the *Mahabharata*. The moon's rays are also said to form, by congelation, the fabulous gem chandrakánta or chandramaṇi. Hémachandra, *Abhidhanaratnamala*, Bk. IV. shl. 133.

60) §. 38. Niebuhr calls the mirror "un petit bouclier;" Goldingham—"a circular shield;" Macneil "a shield or target inverted;" Dr. Hunter—"a small shield" grasped "by that part which is meant for the insertion of the arm;" and with these Erskine agrees. There seems little doubt, however, that Du Perron was correct in calling it "une espece de miroir:" it is a native mirror. Niebuhr, *Voyage*, tom. II. p. 27.; *Asiat. Res.* vol. IV. p. 410; *Archæologia*, vol. VIII. p. 274, and vol. VII. p. 293; *Trans. Lit. Soc. Bomb.* vol. I. p. 221; and Du Perron, *Zendavesta*, vol. I. p. cccexxii.

61) §. 38. Dr. J. Wilson, *u. s.* p. 13; and conf. *Jour. Beng. As. Soc.* vol. VI. pp. 223-225 and 225-230. The bull Nandi is always painted of a milk white colour; thus in the *Meghaduta*:—

"As Shiva's Bull upon his sacred neck,
Amidst his ermine, owns some sable speck;
So shall thy shade upon the mountain show,
Whose sides are silvered with eternal snow."

His image, which always faces the linga, is often placed outside the temple under a separate *mandapa*, and is sometimes of considerable size;—at Hallibedu in Maisur are two images of Nandi—one of them 16 feet long, 10 feet high, and 7 feet broad, and the other not quite so large. In some places in Malabar the bull is the village god, and is there called Basava, a corrupt form of Vṛishabha, and the name of the founder of the Lingáyit sect, by whom Basava is considered an incarnation of Nandi. In Upper India Lingáyit mendicants used, formerly at least, to be met with occasionally leading about a bull, the living type of Nandi, decorated with housings of various colours and strings of *cowri* shells.—H. H. Wilson *Meghaduta*, ll. 359ff, *Works*, vol. IV. p. 361; and vol. I. p. 225; Moor, *Hindu Pantheon*, pp. 36,58; Buchanan, *Jour. through Mysore*, &c. vol. III. pp. 391 92, and 253; Roger, *La Porte ouverte*, p. 207. Nandi is sometimes called Trishingi = three-horned.—*Narmakathakosha*, s. v. Vṛishabha is also the *china* or cognizance of Rishabhanátha, the first Tírthankara of the Jainas. One of the Puránas is the Nandipuráṇa. See note 66.

62) §. 39. The other symbols of Vishnu are the padma or lotus, and the gadá a mace or club. These, however, belong rather to his avatáras or incarnations than to his proper form. Moor, *Hind. Panth.* p. 24. For Vishnu's constant appearance in these sculptures on the left of Shiva, and Brahmá's on the right, we have perhaps the authority in the *Anushasana-parva* of the *Mahabharata*, iv. 869, 875:—"On the right of the god was Brahmá, patriarch of the world, standing on a celestial car, drawn by swans, and fleet as thought. On the left was Náráyana (Vishnu) mounted on Garuḍa bearing a shell, discus and club... The gods then lauded Mahádeva with various hymns. Brahmá celebrated him, reciting the rathantara, while Náráyaṇa hymned the god of gods with the jyeshtha sáman, and Indra uttering that most eminent prayer, the excellent Shatarudriya. Brahmá, Naráyaṇa, and the king of the gods (Indra) the son of Kusíka, the three mighty deities shone like the three fires."—Muir, *Sansk. Texts*, Pt. IV. p. 162.

63) §. 39. See Moor, *Hind. Panth.* p. 98. The legends respecting the monster Garuḍa are wild in the extreme. He was produced, say they, from an egg laid by his mother

Vinatá, and immediately his body expanded till it touched the sky; all the animals were terrified at him ; his eyes were like lightening ; and the mountains were blown away by the wind of his wings ; and the rays that issued from his body set the four quarters of the world on fire. The affrighted gods, thinking he must be an incarnation of Agni, sought the help of the god of fire. His mother Vinatá and Kadru the mother of the serpent race had a dispute about the colour of the horse (*Uchchainshrava*) produced at the churning of the ocean, and Vinatá having laid a wager on it, she lost it through the deception of Kadru, and thereby became her slave. The serpent race becoming desirous of immortality, promised to set her at liberty on condition that Garuḍa should procure them the *amrita* (see note 59). Having obtained it for them, Vinatá was set free, but while they were bathing, before tasting it, the *amrita* was carried off by Indra. Conf. Wilford, *Asiat. Res.* vol. VI. pp. 513, 514 ; *Harivansa* (Langlois transl.) tom. II. p. 79, &c. Moor, *Hind. Panth.* pp. 278, 288, 334, 335 ; Ward, *Hindus*, vol. I. p. 256 ; Wilson, *Vishnu Pur.* (4to. ed.) p. 149, or (8vo. ed.), vol. II. p. 73. Amarasinha calls him Garutmán, Tárkshya, Vainatéya Khageshwara, Nágántika, Vishṇuratha, Suparṇa, and Pannagáshana. According to popular belief the emerald, Gárutmat, is produced from the phlegm expectorated by Garuḍa or Garutman. In the *Ramayana* he is represented as the father of Jatáyus, the chief of the vultures, who lived with Ráma at Panchávati or Náshik. He is one of the Bhuvanapatis of the Jainas. At Kálápáhár near Jájipur Lieut. Kittoe found a fine old image of Garuḍa with small wings, a high cap, and monstrous human nose. See his sketch *Jour. Beng. As. Soc.* vol. VII. (1838) pt. i. pl. 5. p. 55. Conf. D'Herbelot. *s. v.* 'Simorgh' ; *Dabistan*, vol. I. pp. 55, 191, and vol. III. pp. 249, 250 ; Wilson, *Hind. Theat.* vol. I. pp. 34, 131, 304, vol. II. p. 329.

64) §. 39. The Chámara is frequently referred to by the Hindu poets as a symbol of royalty. Thus Kalidasa says,—(*Kumara Sambhava* canto. I. sl. 13)—

" E'en the wild kine that roam his forests bring
The royal-symbols to the Mountain-King,—
With tails outspread, their bushy streaming hair
Flashes like moonlight through the parted air ;
What monarch's fan more glorious might there be,
More meet to wave before such majesty ?"

It is often fixed in a richly ornamented handle, sometimes of gold inlaid with precious stones. And in ancient times the chariot horses of royal personages had *chamaras* fixed between their ears, like the plume of the war horse of chivalry. Thus in Kalidasa's *Vikramurvasi*, King Purúravas says to his charioteer,—

" Bend our course
To yonder point, and urge the rapid steeds
To swiftest flight. 'Tis done ; before the car
Like vollied dust the scattering clouds divide ;
The whirling wheel deceives the dazzled eye,
And double round the axle seems to circle.
The waving *Chaunri* on the steed's broad brow
Points backward, motionless as in a picture ;
And backward streams the banner from the breeze
We meet—immovable."

It is the constant practice of the Hindus to whisk the flies off from the images of their gods with the *Chámara* ; thus in the *Meghaduta* of the same poet, we have—

" They who, with burning feet and aching arms
With wanton gestures and emblazoned charms,

In *Mahadeva's* fane the measure tread,
Or wave the gorgeous *Chaunri* o'er his head."

The Yak is the grunting ox of Tennant, the *Bos poephagus*, *Poephagus grunniens*, or *Bos grunniens*, of naturalists. Conf. *Raja Tarangini*, I. 81 ; V. 449; Griffith, *Birth of the War-God*, p. 3; Wilson, *Hind. Theat.* vol. I. p. 199 ; *Works*, vol. IV. p. 346 ; Langlois, *Harivansa*, tom. I. p. 307.

65) §. 41. Indra was originally the supreme god of the Hindus. He is the regent of the east, and sovereign of the three Lokas. As god of the firmament he is bespangled with stars and varied with every change of cloud,—

"A thousand glorious eyes
Glancing like lillies when the soft wind sighs."

In pictures, his arms and the upper part of his body are represented as full of eyes. Sometimes he has an *ankush* in both hands, and his elephant is represented with three trunks. In the *Veda* he is the son Dyu, the god of light or the sky. The name is derived by Max Müller from the same root with *indu*—drop, sap,—and means originally the giver of rain.—*Lect. on Lang.* 2nd Series, p. 436. Sir W. Jones, *Asiat. Res.* vol. I. p. 241.

66) §. 41. Nandi is also the name of Shiva's favourite attendant, and is mentioned in the *Kumara Sambhava* (see extract §. 50); and in the Prelude to the *Malati Madhava* of Bhavabhuti (8th century), he is alluded to as playing the tabor while Shiva dances the tándava. In the *Bhagavata Purana*, (IV. 220) he is called Nandishwara, and appears at Daksha's sacrifice in defence of his master; and in the *Uttara Kanda* of the *Ramayana*, he is described as "a formidable dark tawny-coloured dwarf," with the face of a monkey. The name Nandi means 'delight.' (See note 61). Nárada is not so probably represented as Nandi. He is often spoken of in connection with Shiva, but belongs to the *gana* of Vishnu rather than of Shiva. He is the son of Brahmá, one of the ten original Munis or Rishis, and the inventor of the Víṇá or lute. Mágha, in his poem on the death of Shishupála, says (ch. I. shl. 4), of Nárada,—"in the midst of huge "clouds, fresh formed, he descended white as a heap of powdered camphor, entirely like "to Shambhu (*Shiva*), of the grey colour of ashes, throwing into the air from time to "time the skin of a great elephant (*in dancing*)." Conf. §. 62 ; Wilson, *Hind. Theat.* vol. I. p. 9 ; *Raja Tarangini*, Bk. I. shl. 36, 123 ; Muir, *Sansk. Texts*, Pt. IV. pp. 319, 393 ; Moor, *Hind. Panth.* p. 204 ; Jones, *Asiat. Res.* vol. I. p. 264.

67) §. 42. The special attendants of Shiva are the Pramathas, and the head of his *gana* is Gaṇesha, but among the *gaṇa* may be reckoned the Kinnaras, the musicians of Swarga and attendants on Kuvera, the god of wealth, from whom—

"Hymns to the victor of Tripura rise."

They have the heads of horses on human bodies, and are so named from *Kim nara*—'what sort of men?' They are fabled to have been produced from the feet of Brahmá, with the Yakshas, Pisháchas, Rákshasas, Bhútas, Gandharvas, &c. Kalidása frequently refers to them : thus in the *Kumara Shambava* (cant. I. shl. 11) he says,—"There upon the ways where the frozen snow chills their heels and toes the wives "of the horse-faced *Kinnaras* cannot quicken their slow step, being impeded with the "heavy burden of their hips and breasts"—which Mr. Griffiths has spiritedly rendered—

"Why lingers yet the heavenly ministrel's bride
On the wild path that skirts Himálaya's side?—
Cold to her tender feet—oh, cold—the snow,
Why are her steps—her homeward steps—so slow?
'Tis that her slender ankles scarce can bear
The weight of beauty that impedes her there."

In shloka 14, he again speaks of them—

"There, where the Nymphs, within the cave's recess,
In modest fear their gentle limbs undress,
Descending clouds hang fondly round to shade
The blushing beauties of each mountain maid."

The Gandharvas are also celestial musicians and form the orchestra at all the festival occasions of the principal deities. The Vidyádharas are male and female dancers. The Apsarases are female dancers celebrated for their beauty, among whom are Urvásí, Ménaká, Rambhá, Punchachúrá, and Tilottamá. Like Aphrodite, they arose from the sea, and derive their name from *ap* 'water,' and *sara* 'who moves.' Their origin is thus related in the first book of the *Ramayana* :—

"Then from the agitated deep upsprung
The legion of Apsarases, so named
That to the watery element they owed
Their being. Myriads were they born, and all
In vesture heavenly clad, and heavenly gems :
Yet more divine their native semblance, rich
With all the gifts of grace, and youth, and beauty.
A train innumerous followed : Yet thus fair
Nor god nor demon sought their wedded love :
Thus, Rághava, they still remain—their charms
The common treasure of the host of heaven."

The Náyikás, Yoginís, &c. are female companions or attendants of Párvatí. Conf. Wilson, *Meghaduta*, *Works* vol. IV. p. 365 ; *Raghuvansa*, ch. iv. shl. 78, ch. vii. shl. 48 ; Lassen, *Zeitschrift f. d. Kunde des Morg.* Bd. II. hf. i. s. 61 ; Ward, *Hindus*, vol. I. pp. 185-192. Tod, *Rajasthan*, vol. II. pp. 706, 750 ; Troyer, *Rajatarangini*, tom. I. p. 416, 425 ; tom. II. p. 24 ; Wilson, *Essays on Sansk. Lit.* vol I. p. 55 ; and *Sansk. Dict.*

68) §. 42. The Munis or sages are frequently introduced in Hindu mythology. By their penances, they are supposed to attain unbounded power :—

"Ancient Creators !—Thus the wise who know,
Gave them a name in ages long ago—
With Brahmá joining in creation's plan,
And perfecting the work his will began ;
Still firm in Penance, though the hermit-vow
Bears a ripe harvest for the sages now."

They are identified with the seven stars of Ursa Major, and are attended by the virtuous Arundhatí the wife of Vasishṭha—corresponding to the small star near one of the most northern. Their names are Maríchi, Vasishṭha, Angiras, Atri, Pulastya, Pulaha, and Kratu. The different *Puranas* vary, however, in their accounts of them. Conf. Wilson, *Essays, on Sansk. Lit.* vol. I. pp. 125, 127, 150 ; *Vishnu Purana*, (4to. ed.) pp. 49, 56, 260-69. or (8vo. ed.) vol. I. pp. 100, 101, 112, vol. III. pp. 6-36 ; Muir, *Sansk. Texts*, vol. I. p. 36 ; Colebrooke, *Essays* vol. I. p. 229 ; vol. II. pp. 352, 355 ; Moor, *Hind. Panth.* pp. 84-91, and 148 ; Griffiths, *u. s.* pp. 4, 56, and 57. See note 82.

69) § 43. Griffiths' transl. *u. s.* p. 14.

70) § 44. Erskine, *ut. sup.* p. 226. Amarasinha (Bk. I. c. ii. sec. 3. shl. 30-31) gives the names of the Gangá and Yamuná as,—

1. Gangá, Viṣhṇupadí, Jahnutanayá, Surnimnagá, Bhágírathí, Tripathagá, Trisrotá, Bhíṣhmasúr-api.
2. Kalindí Súryatnayá, Yamuná, Shamanasvasá.

Tripathagá—Erskine interprets as "going by three roads," but Wilson makes it to mean "flowing through earth, heaven, and hell;" and Trisrotá—"the river of the three worlds, or one with three channels." Conf. Moor, *Hind. Panth.* p. 429, and plate 75, fig. 2; Wilson's Meghaduta, *Essays on Sansk. Lit.* vol. II. pp. 358-60; *Asiat. Res.* vol. XIV. pp. 124, 334, 455; Troyer, *Raja Tarangini*, tom. I. pp. 397, 440, 466, 476; J. Talboys Wheeler, *Hist. Ind.* vol. II. pp. 45, 46.

71) §. 45. Erskine makes the following remarks on the dress:—"It has been observed by some writers, that the dress of the figures is different from that now in use in India; and Niebuhr remarks that the figures are beardless, except that of Shiva in the great bust, to which may be added that in the eastern chapel, and the bearded múnis, which he overlooked. But so far is the observation from being true, that there is not a piece of dress on any figure in the cave, except the fancy cap on some of them, which is not at this day commonly met with in India. The shelá or long web of thin cloth folded round the loins, is that in general use all over Hindustan and the Dekhan. The same may be said of the jewels and ornaments;—they are precisely the heavy tasteless ornaments that load the necks, ankles, arms, and ears of the Hindus. If most of the figures are nearly naked, this is owing to several reasons. Statuaries naturally dislike formal dresses as a great incumbrance on their art, since they conceal or deform the most graceful contours of the human body, the expression of which, and of the emotions of the countenance, is the great triumph of their art. In the next place, there are really very few pieces of genuine Hindu dress: the Brahman, for example, has only the dhotra, or cloth which covers the lower part of the body, and the angavastra, which is wrapped round the upper part of the body;—till he is married, he wears only the angavastra and langoti, which last is a short cloth that passes between the thighs, and is fastened before and behind to a string that goes round the loins: the Sanyási uses an angavastra dyed yellow with saffron and called chháṭí, and the langoti. The Gosávis and Bairágis wear the langoti alone. The only regular parts of the dress of a woman are the lugaḍá, a long web of cloth from 16 to 20 cubits in length, which after covering the middle part of the body is thrown over the shoulders and forms a graceful covering for the upper part; and the choli, a short jacket with short sleeves, used to support rather than to conceal the breast. Most of the articles of dress now worn have been introduced by the Musalmans; such as the angarkhá and dupaṭá, which cover the upper part of the body; the turban, the cholaṇá or short drawers, &c. It should be remembered too, that when a Hindu approaches his gods reverently, he purifies himself, and throws off all his dress except that part which covers his loins, and many of the figures in this cave are in the act of adoration. Finally the principal figures are gods, who in most nations have been represented with little covering. At present, none of the figures in Elephanta are sculptured in a state of entire nudity; though it is said that some of those now broken more nearly approached the state of nature, and were mutilated by the piety or wantonness of visitors. As for the circumstance of the figures being beardless, it is owing to their representing celestial beings, who are supposed to enjoy eternal youth. The múnis or celestial sages, however, are always represented in these sculptures, as they are in the Hindu mythology, with beards, as being aged. Shiva also in Hindu poems, as well as in paintings, has frequently either a beard or mustachios."—*Tr. Bom. Lit. Soc.* vol. I. pp. 243-45.

This is not quite accurate: the Hindu who goes to worship only takes off his turban, but must have on his angavastra (Sansk. uttaríya, Prakrit—uparṇá) and dhotra: the tawny cloth (Sans. sháṭi) of the Sanyásis is stained with *catechu*, not with *saffron:* and, as remarked in the text, most of the figures have the dhotra or lugaḍa; some of the pisháchas have a kaupína or large langoti; and many wear the shelá; the cholí (Sans. chola or kúrpásaka) has been remarked on some of the female figures, and perhaps it is the edge of the chaṇḍátaka or short petticoat worn by women of rank, that has been remarked over the legs of many of the flying female figures. The kamarband is not unfrequent, and it may be remarked that the yadnyopavíta or Brahmanical cord is far thicker than it ever is now-a-days and of a strength and texture quite different. Jewellery is represented in great abundance and variety. All the figures have wristlets, but only the females have anklets.

72) §. 48. Erskine calls this "a conch or spiral shell," and remarks that Mr. Macneil and Dr. Hunter mention it as "a fish,"—which he seems to regard as a gross blunder: the use of a ladder would have convinced Mr. Erskine that he was as much in error as his predecessors. Conf. *Trans. Lit. Soc. Bomb.* vol. I. p. 225.

73) §. 49. It is remarkable that Erskine should have felt unable to agree with his predecessors, Pyke, Macneil, Hunter, and Major Moor, that this really represents a marriage. For an account of the marriage ceremonies of the Hindus, see Colebrooke, *Essays*, vol. I. pp. 203, 224.

74) §. 50. See note 68.

75) §. 50. Griffiths, *ut sup.* pp. 67ff., and compare the account in the *Shiva Purana*, quoted in the notes to Southey's *Curse of Kehama*, canto x.

76) §. 53. *Jour. Bomb. B. R. As. Soc.* vol IV. p. 273.

77) §. 53. Griffiths's transl. *ut sup.* pp. 78, 79.

78) §. 54. Ibid., and conf. *Asiat. Res.* vol. I. p. 262.

79) §. 56. In the *Meghaduta*, Kalidasa describes Mahásena as—

"Son of the Crescent's god, whom holy ire
Called from the flame of all-devouring fire,
To snatch the lord of Swarga from despair,
And timely save the trembling hosts of air."

On this passage Professor Wilson remarks,—"Several instances of solitary production of offspring occur in the Hindu as well as in the Grecian mythology. Thus, as Pallas sprang from the brow of Jupiter, we have Skanda generated solely by the deity Shiva; Gangá springs from the head of the same deity; and Gaṇesha is the self-born son of the goddess Párvatí.... The germ of Skanda was cast by Shiva into the flame of Agni, the god of fire; who, being unable to sustain the increasing burden, transferred it to the goddess Gangá: she accordingly was delivered of the deity Skanda, who was afterwards received and reared, among thickets of the Shara reed (*Saccarum Sara*), by the six daughters of a king named Kṛittiká; or according to other legends, by the wives of the seven great Ṛishis or saints. In either case they form the asterism of the Pleiades. Upon his coming to maturity, Skanda encountered and killed the demon Táraka, who had filled the region of Indra with dismay:—

Emissumque emâ de sede Typhoëa terrâ,
Cœlitibus fecisse metum."

This is not quite in accordance with the *Kumara Sambhava*, which makes him at least the foster son of Umá, as does also the *Anandalahari*. Conf. note 85; Wilson, *Essays on Sansk. Liter.* vol. II. pp. 352-53; Moor, *Hindu Panth.* pp. 53 and 176; Ward, *Hindus*, vol. I. pp. 60-64; Coleman, *Hindu Mythology*, pp. 74 78; Troyer, *Raja Tarangini*, tom. I. p. 334; *Amarakosha*, Bk. I. ch. I. sec. 1. shl. 34-36.

80) §. 56. Griffiths, *ut sup.* pp. 19, 20.

81) §. 57. *Jour. Bomb. B. R. As. Soc.* vol. IV. p. 273.

82 §. 58. Bhringi is a leading member of the gaṇa of Shiva. He is also called Náḍídeha, Náḍívigraha, and Náḍísneha. In the *Bálá Rámáyana* (Anka. ii. shl. 1-2) we are told that 'Bhringi Rishi wore a kaupinácchhádana, or langoti of the bark of trees, necklaces of rudráksha, his hair matted in a jaṭa, a rudrankusha in his hand, and the tripuṇḍra; and his bones were seen fastened together by the muscles.'—This extract is due to Dr. Bhau Daji, to whom I am also indebted for some other suggestions.

83) §. 59. Kailása :—with this name compare the Greek κοῖλος, and the Latin Coelum, in Ennius written Coelus. It is placed among the Himálaya mountains: it is the site of Alaká, the capital of Kuvera, the god of wealth, and the favourite haunt of Shiva. Conf. Wilson, *Vish. Pur.* (4to ed.) p. 172, or (8vo. ed.) vol. II. p. 123; *Essays on Sansk. Lit.* vol. II. pp. 368, 369; Southey, *Curse of the Kehama*, canto xix. note. Troyer, *Raja Tarangini*, tom. II. pp. 302, 303.

84) §. 60. *Trans. Lit Soc. Bomb.* vol. I. p. 229.

85) §. 61. The following is an outline of the story of Rávaṇa's visit to Kailása as given in the *Ramayana* (VII. xvi. 1-43): "After his victory over Kuvera, Rávaṇa went to Sharavaṇa, the birth place of Kárttikéya. Ascending the mountain he sees another delightful wood, where his car *Pushpaka* stops, and will proceed no further. He then sees a formidable dark tawny-coloured dwarf called Nandíshvara, a follower of Mahádeva, who desires him to halt, as that deity is sporting on the mountain, and has made it inaccessible to all creatures, the gods included. Rávaṇa angrily demands who Shankara is, and laughs contemptuously at Nandíshvara, who has the face of a monkey. Nandíshvara, who was another body of Shiva, being incensed at this contempt of his monkey form, declares that beings, possessing the same shape as himself, and of similar energy, monkeys, shall be produced to destroy Rávaṇa's race. Nandíshvara adds that he could easily kill Rávaṇa now, but that he has been already slain by his own deeds. Rávaṇa threatens that as his car has been stopped, he will pluck up the mountain by the roots, asking in virtue of what power Shiva continually sports on that spot, and boasting that he must now be made to know his danger. Rávaṇa then throws his arms under the mountain, which being lifted by him, shakes, and makes the hosts of Rudra tremble, and even Párvatí herself quake, and cling to her husband. Shiva however presses down the mountain with his great toe, and along with it crushes the arms of Rávaṇa, who utters a loud cry, which shakes all creation. Rávaṇa's councillors then exhort him to propitiate Mahádeva, the blue-throated lord of Umá, who on being lauded will become gracious. Rávaṇa accordingly praises Mahádeva with hymns, and weeps for a thousand years. Mahádeva is then propitiated, lets go Rávaṇa's arms, says his name shall be Rávaṇa from the cry (*rava*) he had uttered, and sends him away with the gift of a sword bestowed on him at his request."—Muir, *Sansk. Texts*, Pt. IV. p. 393. Conf. *Trans. Lit. Soc. Bomb.* vol. I. pp. 42, 43; vol. III. p. 296; *Jour. Bomb. B. R. A. Soc.* vol. IV. pp. 267 and 273; Moor, *Hind. Panth.* p. 338.

86) §. 62. Shiva is called Kapálí, because he wears a necklace of human skulls; some accounts say the skulls are those of giants or asuras,—from *kapála*, a skull.

87) §. 62. De Couto (*ut. sup.* p. 253) says,—"A quarta mão direita com a parte do braço está quebrada pela travessura dos soldados que alli vam das Armadas, como o está quasi tudo." This is the compartment which Capt. Pyke "looked upon as the story of Solomon's Wisdom," and Capt. Grose agreed with him; but respecting this opinion Mr. Macneil asks—"Where are the two women by whose conduct he was to detect imposition,

and where have we ever heard that Solomon had *eight hands* and eight arms?" *Archæologia*, vol. VII. p. 326; vol. VIII. p. 277; Grose, *Voyage*, vol. I. p. 61. Conf. Erskine *ut sup.* pp. 229, 230; and *Trans. R. Asiat. Soc.* vol. II. p. 326.

88) §. 62. Part of Shiva's scanty raiment is the skin of an elephant, or more properly of an Asura or Titan killed by him under that form, and thence named Gajásura. Autumn with its Kásha grass, &c., is thus compared with Shiva's dress in the *Mudrâ Rákshasa*—

"Like Shiva's ashen whiteness, autumn bears
The budding grass, and like the foul hide wears
The dun clouds, scattering from the silver beams
Of the bright moon—that in mid azure gleams,
As on his polished brow—
Above, below,
O'er all, they twine;
More brilliant than around his neck the line
Of the skull-woven chaplet—see—on high,
You row of swans sail laughing through the sky,
The godhead's pearly smile.—May Autumn, clad
In Shiva's semblance, thus make glad
The hearts of men."

See Wilson, *Hind. Theat.* vol. II. pp. 58, 59, 196; *Works*, vol. IV. pp. 347-48; see a prose version of the extract in the text from *Malati Madhava*, in Colebrooke, *Essays*, vol. II. p. 143; and conf. Troyer, *Raja Tarangini*, tom. I. pp. 427-28.

89) §. 63. Muir, *Sansk. Texts*, Pt. IV. pp. 314ff.

90) §. 63. Conf. *Jour. Bomb. B. R. A. Soc.* vol. IV. pp. 268, 273-74; Erskine, *u. s.* pp. 229-30; Dr. J. Wilson, *Cal. Rev.* vol. XLII. pp. 13, 14; Maurice, *Ind. Antiq.* vol. I. pp. cii, 253.

91) §. 64. Muir, *Sansk. Texts*, Pt. IV. p. 319.

92) §. 64. *Asiatic Researches*, vol. V. pp. 371-91; Dr. J. Wilson, *India Three Thousand Years Ago*, p. 68; H. H. Wilson, *Works*, vol. I. pp. 21, 264; vol. II. pp. 247-69; and conf. Max Muller, *Hist. Sansk. Lit.* p. 408; Muir, *Sansk. Texts*, vol. I. p. 11; Buchanan, *Jour. through Mysore*, vol. I. p 319. The Kápálika is thus described in the *Shankara Vijaya* of Anandagiri :—" His body is smeared with ashes from a funeral pile, around his neck hangs a string of human skulls, his forehead is streaked with a black line, his hair is wove into the matted braid, his loins are clothed with a tiger's skin, a hollow skull is in his left hand (for a cup), and in his right he carries a bell, which he rings incessantly, exclaiming aloud, Ho! Shambhu, Bhairava—Ho lord of Kálí!"

93) §. 64. Literally 'with the collyrium of *Yoga*.'

94) §. 64. *Journal Beng. As. Soc.* vol. VI. pp. 14, 15. Conf. Taylor, *Prabodha Chandrodaya*, pp. 38, 39; and Brockhaus, *Prabodh. Chand.* p. 53.

95) §. 66. The Omkára or Praṇava, written ओम् or ओं='om' is 'the mystic name of the deity prefacing all prayers and most of the writings of the Hindus,' from अ=*a*—a name of Vishṇu, उ=*u*—of Shiva, and म=*m*—of Brahmá; it therefore implies the Indian *triad*.—H. H. Wilson, *Sansk. Dict.* For some curious information on this mystical syllable, see H. H. Wilson, *Works*, vol. I. pp. 4, 81, 223; *Vishnu Purana*, (4to. ed.) pp. 1, 273, 274; Colebrooke, *Essays*, vol. I. pp. 130, 210, 251, 344, 407; Paterson, *Asiat. Res.* vol. VIII. p. 62; Moor, *Hind. Panth.* pp. 409, 414, 443; Laidlay, *Foe-koe-ki*, p. 91; Langlois, *Harivansa*, tom. II. p. 325; Cunningham, *Bhilsa Topes*, pp. 355-61; Fergusson, *Tree and*

Serpent Worship, p. 106; Muir, *Sansk. Texts*, Vol. III. p. 44; *Bhagavata Gitá*, XVII. shl. 23; *Menu*, II. shl. 76ff; Maurice, *Ind. Antiq.* vol. I. pp. 201, 397; vol. IV. p. 744; *Asiat. Res.* vol. I. p. 242; King, *Gnostics*, p. 163; Vassilief, *Le Bouddisme*, p. 182.

The figure in this sculpture recurs in the fifth compartment several times, but with the curve in the middle considerably modified, and in one case turned in the opposite direction, and in another, the cross above is more developed. At Elurá it occurs over one of Rávaṇa's hands, with a face in the centre—a modified form of the *Kirttimukha;* and in a cave at Kolhapur it appears with a distinct cross, but without any curve in the middle. Conf. Erskine, *u. s.* pp. 230, 231; Stevenson, *u. s.* p. 268; Dr. J. Wilson, *Cal. Rev.* vol. XLII. p. 14; *Jour. Bomb. B. R. As. Soc.* vol. IV. p. 363; Moor, *Hind. Panth.* p. 50.

96) §. 68. *Archæologia*, vol. VII. p. 287; *Trans. Lit. Soc. Bomb.* vol. I. p. 236; *Da Asia u. s.* tom. VII. pp. 251-2; De Coutto's words are,—"Dentro no corpo della estam "multos idolos, e no meio da Capella se vê hum de altura de dezesete palmos, com huma "grande, e formosa tiara na cabeça, lavrada de tantas laçarias, lavores, e subtilezas, que "mais parecem debuxadas, que entalhadas em pedra com escopro. Tem esta figura oito "braços, e só duas pernas. Em huma das mãos direitas tem hum sceptro alevantado, "e nelle enroscada huma cobra de capello, assim como pintam o de Mercurio."

97) §. 69. *Jour Bomb. B. R. As. Soc.* vol. IV. p. 274.

98) §. 69. Two kinds of dance are mentioned in Sanskrit works:—1. Lásya—said to have been invented by Párvatí and communicated by her to Uṣhá the daughter of Báṇásura, by whom her companions and the Gopis of Dwáraká were instructed in it; and by them it was communicated to the women of Suráshtra: it is the nách or dance practised by females, gentle in its movements, and consisting largely in attitudes and gesticulation. 2. Táṇḍava—a frantic dance with violent gesticulation, of which there are said to be two varieties: one of them is performed by Shiva at eventide (*sayamkála*) to the sound of his musical instruments, with his hair loose, stamping with frantic energy, attended by his gaṇa and Pisháchas, when the dust he raises is put on their heads by the other devatas; the other is performed when, in sport, he destroys the world,—fixing the elephants of the four corners on his trishula, and dancing wildly. This dance is frequently referred to by the poets. It is vividly described in the extract given in §. 62. In the same poem we find another allusion to it, in the soliloquy of Kapálakundalá,—

———"The hollow skulls,
That low descending from my neck depend,
Emit fierce music as they clash together,
Or strike the trembling plates that gird my loins,
Loose stream on every side my woven locks
In lengthening braids;—upon my pond'rous staff,
The string of bells, light waving to and fro,
Jangles incessantly;—my banner floats
Upborne upon the wailing breeze, whose tone
Is deepened by the echoes it awakes
Amidst the caverns of each fleshless skull,
That hangs in dread array around my person."

See Wilson, *Hindu Theatre*, vol. I. p. xix; vol. II. pp. 53, 153; and conf. Troyer, *Raja Tarangini*, tom. I. p. 401.

99) §. 71. *Kumara Sambhava*, Sarg. ix. shl. 48, 49.

100) §. 72. *Da Asia* u. s. tom. vii. p. 252 :—"hum idolo de hum só corpo com tres cabeças, e em cada huma dellas tem hum só braço, salvo a do meio, que tem dous, e na esquerda tem hum livro."

101) §. 73. This sculpture is repeated with but slight variations of detail in the portico of the west wing of the Cave (see §. 91). A similar figure also occurs in the Dumár Lená cave at Elurá, where it is locally styled Dharma Rája or 'Jám Dharma.' For this Col. Sykes could give no more satisfactory account than Erskine had done of the Elephanta sculpture in supposing it 'was borrowed directly from the Bauddha sect, or that there was anciently an attempt to unite the Bauddhas to the sect of Shiva.' Hindu literature, however, abounds with accounts of the ascetic austerities of Shiva: Kálidása with his usual poetical refinement introduces his account of the great Yogi in the lines,—

"Then the great deity who gives the prize
Of penance, prayer, and holy exercise,
As though to earn the meed he grants to man,
Himself the penance and the pain began."

This devotion of Shiva to Yoga is alluded to in the benediction with which the *Toy Cart* opens:—"May that profound meditation of Shambhu protect you! which is intent on Brahme, the absorbing end of every effort of abstract vision; as he contemplates with the eye of wisdom, spirit, in himself, detached from all material instruments; his senses being restrained by holy knowledge, as he sits ruminating with suspended breath, whilst his serpents coil with the folds of his vesture round his bended knees." Yoga is ascribed to Shiva, who taught it in the person of Shweta on the Himálaya mountains in the beginning of the Káli age. Sykes, *Tr. Bom. Lit. Soc.* vol. III. pp. 273, 317; Erskine, *ib.* vol. I. p. 232; *Birth of the War-god,* u. s. p. 11; Wilson, *Hind. Theat.* vol. I. p. 13; *Works,* vol. I. pp. 210, 211; *Asiat. Res.* vol. XVII. p. 183.

102) §. 74. The superstition of the Hindus has led them to invent particular attitudes for the performance of the various acts of devotion: they enumerate as many as eighty-four. Niebuhr remarks that to show the soles of the feet, as is done by this statue, is esteemed by orientals as disrespectful. This remark, however, would not apply to a *Yogi.* There is a figure of Buddha at Kárlá and others at Kanheri and Násik that bear a close analogy to this one of Maháyogi. Niebuhr, *Voy.* tom. II. p. 30; Erskine, *u. s.* p. 236. Conf. Moor, *Hind. Panth.* pp. 245, 246, and plate 72; Salt, *Trans. Lit. Soc. Bomb.* vol. I. p. 48.

103) §. 74. *Birth of the War-god,* p. 27.

104) §. 75. *Ibid.* pp. 10, 11, and 23. In illustration of this compartment, Dr. Stevenson remarks that the whole of the 22nd Adhyáya of the *Linga Purana* is important. "It is a section," he writes, "which describes prophetically the spiritual worship of Shiva, and the ascetic forms he assumes in all the twenty-eight Manwantaras, when, seated amid his four sons, forming a group like the five Dhyáni Buddhas, he spends his time in mental contemplation. Shiva, it is said, will in the ninth *manwantara* be called Ṛishabha; now Ṛishabha was a Hindu ascetic king, whom the Jainas claim as their first Tirthankara. In the tenth, it is said, he will be a Muni, seated on the top of the Himálayas. In the fourteenth, it is said, he will be called Gautama and sit in the *Gautama Vana.* Gautama is both the name of a Hindu sage and of the last Buddha, but the attitude and place lead us to think the latter rather than the former, though the author probably wished his readers to understand the Brahman Gautama. In the eighteenth, he will be Shikhandi, *i. e.* 'feather-crested,' whence a sect of Gosains derive their peculiar badge. In the twelfth he is to be called Arti, and cover himself

with ashes, as a large sect of Gosains do. In the seventeenth, he is to be called Guhavási, *i.e.* 'inhabitant of the Cave,' and to sit in a cave of the Himálaya Mountains." *Jour. Bomb. B. R. As. Soc.* vol. IV. p. 274, 275.

105) §. 76. The Rudráksha is the *Eleocarpus ganitrus* of Roxburgh. Among the forms of adoration which are constantly employed by the worshippers of Shiva is the *japa*, or muttered recitation of his different names as the worshipper turns between his fingers the beads of a rosary (málá), made of the seeds of the Rudráksha. The fullest string contains 108 beads, for each of which there is a separate appellation, as Shiva, Rudra, Hara, &c. The Lingáyits wear necklaces, and carry rosaries of the seeds; the Súkharas—another sect of Shaivas—wear earrings of them; and the Vámis, a sect of Sháktas, use a rosary of them or of coral beads, but of no greater length than may be concealed in the hand, or they keep it in a small purse or a bag of red cloth. Wilson, *Works*, vol. I. pp. 224, 236, 262, and vol II. p. 216.

106) §. 76. Erskine remarks of this figure,—"It may be the same griffin-like animal represented in compartment No. 4 [the *makara* in the *Ardhanarishwara* sculpture]: if it represent a horse, it is the only figure of that noble animal which appears in these sculptures." Moor calls it "a quadruped of equivocal species; its hoofs are discernible, and it may be a horse." It is difficult to understand how any one could doubt its being a horse unless from imperfect examination. *Trans. Lit. Soc. u. s.* p. 232; *Hind. Panth.* p. 246.

107) §. 89. Erskine remarks (*u. s.* p. 235) that "several circumstances seem to indicate that it had once a roof composed of the rock, which has now fallen in and added to the mass of rubbish." What the indicatory circumstances were it is difficult to conjecture: there seems no reason to suppose it was ever otherwise than as stated in the text.

108) §. 89. So much was the court in front of the cistern filled up with rubbish in Erskine's time that he was doubtful "whether it was intended for a covered tank or not." In the plan attached to his memoir, there are four pillars marked in the cistern, though his account is correct enough in stating that there are only two. Erskine, *u. s.* p. 235; De Couto, *DaAsia*, *u.s.* p. 255.

109) §. 95. *DaAsia*, *u. s.* pp. 251, 258, 259.

Before leaving the Great Cave, it may be added here that some time before Mr. Erskine wrote his account, a large fragment of the capitals of one of the pilasters in the south end of the eastern portico fell down. "On examining it," he says, "it appeared to have been fixed on by two large pegs or pins, and the capital being examined, two pieces of teak-wood by which it had been fastened were discovered. It is remarkable, that these pieces of wood when cut with a knife were still very hard and sound within, though they must probably have upheld the fragment for many hundred years." A portion of each of these pegs is still firmly fixed in the pilaster, and the wood is remarkably hard. See *Tr. Lit. Soc. Bom.* vol. I. p. 248.

110) §. 97. This door in some degree resembles that of Cave IV at Ajaṇṭá.

111) §. 101. This is probably the rock-temple about which Niebuhr writes,—"The people say that not far from this is another small *Pagoda* hewn out in a rock; but I did not see it, for there is no open path to it, and the vegetation was then so tall that my guides were afraid of serpents or other wild animals."—*Voyage*, tom. II. p. 33. Conf. Dr. J. Wilson, *Jour. Bomb. B. R. As. Soc.* vol. III. pt. ii. p. 42.

Vetála is generally in the Dekhan said to be an avatára of Shiva, and his exploits are related in the *Vetala Pachisi*. He has no image, however, nor temple, and is worshipped in the open air, generally under the shade of a wide spreading tree;

sometimes, however, he is personified and represented as a human figure with two arms, and worshipped in a temple with the other village gods. He is also one of the *gaṇa* of Shiva, and a demon who haunts cimeteries and animates corpses. Chaṇḍí is a form of Durgá or Párvatí, of whom images are not usually made. Stevenson, *Jour. R. Asiat. Soc.* vol. V. pp. 192-195; Ward, *Hindus*, vol. I. p. 140; Moor, *Hind. Panth.* pp. 118, 145, 146.

The year before last a small seal for a ring was found at the excavations on the east side of the island. It is an oval light ruby coloured carnelian 0·435 inch long by 0·35 inch broad. The length of the face 0·40 and its breadth 0·28 inch, on this is sunk an ellipse 0·37 by 0·26 inch, inside which is sunk characters that stamp the word Náráyaṇa (नारायण) in letters of the 5th or 6th century. It is now in possession of Dr. Bháu Dájí. The accompanying woodcut represents the impression thrice the original size.